Meditation:

Man-Perfection in God-Satisfaction

Sri Chinmoy

Library of Congress Catalog Card no. 80-65399

ISBN 0-88497-444-8

Printed and Published by
AUM PUBLICATIONS
86-24 Parsons Blvd.
Jamaica, N.Y. 11432

Editors' Note

The main text of this book is drawn from the hundreds of extemporaneous talks and answers to questions that Sri Chinmoy has given over the past twenty-five years. Interspersed are some of his inspirational poems and aphorisms.

In selecting and organising this material, we have tried to reflect basic concerns of all those who have embarked on the meditation journey, and in order to make it more accessible to you, we have created the chapter titles and section headings. The special "How To" sections and extensive index are intended to help you develop your own meditation practice, especially if you are a beginner.

In using this book it is best to keep in mind that the same question may be answered in many different ways, depending upon who has asked the question and the particular circumstances involved. Although we have tried to choose the most general answers, every answer may not apply in your specific case. If you are in doubt, the best authority is your own heart. The book is intended to guide and inspire you and not to lay down rules. It is our hope that this book will serve as a valuable friend to you in your spiritual search.

Table of
Contents

Meditation tells us only one thing:
God is. Meditation reveals to us
only one truth: ours is the vision of God.

Meditation: The Language of God

Meditation: The Language of God

❦ Why Do We Meditate?

Why do we meditate? We meditate because this world of ours has not been able to fulfil us. The so-called peace that we feel in our day-to-day life is five minutes of peace after ten hours of anxiety, worry and frustration. We are constantly at the mercy of the negative forces that are all around us: jealousy, fear, doubt, worry, anxiety and despair. These forces are like monkeys. When they get tired of biting us and take rest for a few minutes, then we say that we are enjoying peace. But this is not real peace at all, and the next moment they will attack us again.

It is only through meditation that we can get lasting peace, divine peace. If we meditate soulfully in the morning and receive peace for only one minute, that one minute of peace will permeate our whole day. And when we have a meditation of the highest order, then we get really abiding peace, light and delight. We need meditation because we want to grow in light and fulfil ourselves in light. If this is our aspiration, if this is our thirst, then meditation is the only way.

If we feel that we are satisfied with what we have and what we are, then there is no need for us to enter into the field of meditation. The reason we enter into meditation is because we have an inner hunger. We feel that within us there is something luminous, something vast, something divine. We feel that we need this thing very badly; only right now we do not have access to it. Our inner hunger comes from our spiritual need.

Meditation is not an escape

If we enter into the life of meditation in order to escape from the world and forget our sufferings, then we are doing it for the wrong reason. If we enter into the spiritual life because of outer frustration or dissatisfaction, then we may not remain in the spiritual life. Today I have failed to satisfy my desires; so I am dissatisfied with the world. But tomorrow I will say, "Let me try again. Perhaps this time I will get satisfaction." But eventually we will feel that the desire-life will never satisfy us; we will feel the need to enter into the inner life. This is aspiration.

> *What is meditation? Meditation is man's self-awakening and God's Self-offering. When man's self-awakening and God's Self-offering meet together, man becomes immortal in the inner world and God becomes fulfilled in the outer world.*

In the life of aspiration, we want only God. If we sincerely want God, then naturally He will give Himself to us. But He will do it in His own way and at His own time. If we pray and meditate with sincere aspiration for certain qualities, even if God does not grant them to us, still we will be satisfied. We will simply say, "He knows best. Right now I am not ready for these things. But He will definitely give them to me the day I am ready." In the life of aspiration it is not our achievement that gives us satisfaction; it is our aspiration. Aspiration itself is our satisfaction.

Conscious aspiration and effort

Spirituality cannot be achieved by pulling or pushing. We cannot pull down spiritual light by hook or by crook. When it comes down on its own, only on the strength of our aspiration will we be able to receive it. If we try to pull the light beyond our capacity of receptivity, our inner vessel will break. How do we receive this light from above? How do we expand our consciousness so that our receptivity will increase? The answer is meditation.

Meditation does not mean just sitting quietly for five or ten minutes. It requires conscious effort. The mind has to be made calm and quiet. At the same time, it has to be vigilant so as not to allow any distracting thoughts or desires to enter. When we can make the mind calm and quiet, we will feel that a new creation is dawning inside us. When the mind is vacant and tranquil and our whole existence becomes an empty vessel, our inner being can invoke infinite peace, light and bliss to enter into the vessel and fill it. This is meditation.

> *Meditation is the language of God. If we want to know what God's Will is in our life, if we want God to guide us, mould us and fulfil Himself in and through us, then meditation is the language that we must use.*

When we think that it is we who are trying to meditate, then meditation seems complicated. But real meditation is not done by us. It is done by our Inner Pilot, the Supreme, who is constantly meditating in and through us. We are just the vessel, and we are allowing Him to fill us with His whole Consciousness. We start with our own personal effort, but once we go deep within, we see that it is not our effort that is allowing us to enter into meditation. It is the Supreme who is meditating in and through us with our conscious awareness and consent.

Each person's soul has its own way of meditating. My way of meditating will not suit you, and your way of meditating will not suit me. There are many seekers whose meditation is not fruitful because they are not doing the meditation that is right for them. If you do not have a spiritual Master who can guide you, then you have to go deep within and get your meditation from the inmost recesses of your heart.

This is very difficult for a beginner. You have to go deep, deep within and see if you get a voice or thought or idea. Then you have to go deep into this voice or thought and see if it gives you a feeling of inner joy or peace, where there are no questions or problems or doubts. Only when you get this kind of feeling, can you know that the voice that you have heard is the real inner voice which will help you in your spiritual life.

But if you have a teacher who is a realised soul, his silent gaze will teach you how to meditate. A Master does not have to explain outwardly how to meditate, or give you a specific technique of meditation. He will simply meditate on you and inwardly teach you how to meditate. Your soul will enter into his soul and learn from his soul. All real spiritual Masters teach meditation in silence.

The ultimate aim of meditation is to establish our conscious union with God. We are all God's children, but right now we do not have conscious oneness with God. Someone may believe in God, but this belief is not a reality in his life. He just believes in God because some saint or Yogi or spiritual Master has said there is a God, or because he has read about God in spiritual books. But if we practise meditation, a day comes when we establish our conscious oneness with God. At that time, God gives us His infinite peace, infinite light and infinite bliss, and we grow into this infinite peace, light and bliss.

Meditation: The Language of God

Q&A

Q How does one meditate?

A There are two ways to meditate. One way is to silence the mind. An ordinary man feels that if he silences the mind, he becomes a fool. He feels that if the mind does not think, the mind has lost everything. But this is not true in the spiritual life. In the spiritual life, when we silence the mind we see that a new creation, a new promise to God, dawns in the mind. Right now we have not fulfilled our promise to God; we have not totally dedicated our existence to God. When we can silence the mind, we are in a position to please and fulfil God.

Another way to meditate is to empty the heart. Right now the heart is full of emotional turmoil and problems caused by the impure vital which has enveloped it. The heart is a vessel. Right now this vessel is full of undivine things, things that limit and bind us. If we can empty the heart-vessel, there is someone who will fill it with divine peace, light and bliss, which will liberate us. When we empty our heart of ignorance, God's Wisdom-Light will come and fill it.

Q If a person does not believe in God, can he practise meditation?

A If a person does not believe in God, he can practise meditation but he may not achieve anything. Meditation is the path that leads to God. If you do not believe in God, then naturally you will not follow that path.

Q Is meditation the highest reality?

A You can say that for a beginner meditation is the highest reality. But when one becomes an advanced seeker, one knows that meditation only leads to the highest reality. If someone has been living in ignorance, if he has never prayed or meditated in his life even for a minute, for him meditation is naturally the highest reality that his consciousness can achieve. But when he has practised meditation for a few years, he knows that meditation itself is not the highest reality. The highest reality is something he achieves or grows into by walking along the path of meditation.

Q As one evolves spiritually and achieves realisation, does the focus of his meditation change?

A After one has achieved realisation, it is not necessary for him to meditate the way a seeker meditates. When someone has attained realisation, which is oneness with the Supreme, his meditation is continuous. When a seeker has realised God, he does not meditate to achieve something or to go beyond something. He meditates to bring down peace, light and bliss for humanity or to awaken the consciousness of others.

From the spiritual point of view, every seeker is a beginner. The moment you want to make constant and continual progress, at that moment you become an eternal beginner.

First Things First: How to Begin

First Things First: How to Begin

💥 How Do I Start?

From the spiritual point of view, every seeker is a beginner. A beginner is he who has the inner urge to grow into something ever more divine, ever more illumining and ever more fulfilling. The moment you want to make constant and continuous progress, the moment you want to surpass yourself and enter into the ever-transcending Beyond, at that moment you become an eternal beginner.

If you are an absolute beginner, then you can start by reading a few spiritual books or scriptures. These will give you inspiration. You should read books by spiritual Masters in whom you have implicit faith. There *are* Masters who have attained the highest consciousness, and if you read their books, you are bound to get inspiration. It is better not to read books written by professors or scholars or aspirants who are still on the path and have not yet attained illumination. Only those who have realised the Truth will have the capacity to offer the Truth. Otherwise, it is like the blind leading the blind.

It is also a good idea to associate with people who have been meditating for some time. These people may not be in a position to teach you, but they will be able to inspire you. Even if you just sit beside them while they are meditating, unconsciously your inner being will derive some meditative power from them. You are not stealing anything; only your inner being is taking help from them without your outer knowledge.

In the beginning you should not even think about meditation. Just try to set aside a certain time of day when you will try to be calm and quiet, and feel that these five minutes belong to your inner being and to nobody else. Regularity is of paramount importance. What you need is regular practice at a regular time.

 Every day there is only one thing to learn: how to be honestly happy.

Some basic techniques
For a beginner it is better to start with concentration. Otherwise, the moment you try to make your mind calm and vacant, millions of uncomely thoughts will enter into you and you will not be able to meditate even for one second. If you concentrate, at that time you challenge the wrong thoughts that are trying to enter you. So in the beginning just practise concentration for a few minutes. Then, after a few weeks or a few months, you can try meditation.

When you start meditating, always try to feel that you are a child. When one is a child, one's mind is not developed. At the age of twelve or thirteen, the mind starts functioning on an intellectual level. But before that, a child is all heart. A child feels that he does not know anything. He does not have any preconceived ideas about meditation and the spiritual life. He wants to learn everything fresh.

First feel that you are a child, and then try to feel that you are standing in a flower garden. This flower garden is your heart. A child can play in a garden for hours. He goes from this flower to that flower, but he does not leave the garden, because he gets joy from the beauty and fragrance of each flower. Feel that inside you is a garden, and you can stay in it for as long as you want. In this way you can learn to meditate in the heart.

If you can remain in the heart, you will begin to feel an inner cry. This inner cry, which is aspiration, is the secret of meditation. When an adult person cries, his cry is usually not sincere. But when a child cries, even if he is crying only for candy, he is very sincere. At that time, candy is the whole world for him. If you give him a hundred-dollar bill, he will not be satisfied; he cares only for candy. When a child cries, immediately his father or mother comes to him. If you can cry from deep within for peace, light and truth, and if this is the only thing that will satisfy you, then God your eternal Father and eternal Mother is bound to come and help you.

You should always try to feel that you are as helpless as a child. As soon as you feel that you are helpless, somebody will come to help you. If a child is lost in the street and he begins to cry, some kind-hearted person will show him where his home is. Feel that you are lost in the street and that there is a storm raging. Doubt, fear, anxiety, worry, insecurity and other undivine forces are pouring down on you. But if you cry sincerely, somebody will come to rescue you and show you how to get to your home, which is your heart. And who is that somebody? It is God, your Inner Pilot.

Early in the morning invite God your Friend, your real Friend, your only Friend, to walk along with you during the entire day.

The Inner Pilot
God can appear with form and without form. But during your meditation, it is best to think of the Supreme as a human being. The beginner should always meditate on the personal God. Otherwise, if you try to see God

in His impersonal aspect, you will be confused by His immensity. So start with the personal God and from there you can go to the impersonal God.

Today you may be a beginner in the spiritual life, but do not feel that you will always be a beginner. At one time everybody was a beginner. If you practise concentration and meditation regularly, if you are really sincere in your spiritual search, then you are bound to make progress. The important thing is not to be discouraged. God-realisation does not come overnight. If you meditate regularly and devotedly, if you can cry for God like a child cries for his mother, then you will not have to run to the goal. No, the goal will come and stand right in front of you and claim you as its own, very own.

How To

1 **Simplicity, sincerity, purity.** There are quite a few meditation exercises a beginner can try. For the seeker wishing to enter the spiritual life, simplicity, sincerity, purity and surety are of utmost importance. It is simplicity that grants you peace of mind. It is sincerity that makes you feel that you are of God and that God is constantly for you. It is your pure heart that makes you feel at every moment that God is growing, glowing and fulfilling Himself inside you. It is surety that makes you feel that meditation is absolutely the right thing.

In silence kindly repeat the word "simplicity" inside your mind seven times and concentrate on the crown of your head. Then repeat the word "sincerity" seven times silently and soulfully inside your heart, and concentrate on your heart. Then kindly repeat the word "purity" seven times inside or around your navel centre, and concentrate on the navel centre. Please do all this silently and most soulfully. Then focus your attention on the third eye, which is between and slightly above the eyebrows, and silently repeat "surety" seven times. Next, place your hand on top of your head and say three times, "I am simple, I am simple, I am simple." Then place your hand on your heart and say three times, "I am sincere, I am sincere, I am sincere." Then place your hand on the navel centre, repeating "I am pure," and on the third eye, repeating "I am sure."

2 **A favourite quality.** If you like a particular aspect of God—love, for instance—please inwardly repeat the word "love" most soulfully several times. While uttering the word "love" most soulfully, try to feel it reverberating in the inmost recesses of your heart: "love, love, love." If you care more for divine peace, then please inwardly chant or repeat to yourself the word "peace." While doing this, try to hear the cosmic sound that the word embodies reverberating in the very depths of your heart. If you want light, then please repeat "light, light, light," most soulfully, and feel that you have actually become light. From the soles of your feet to the crown of your head, try to feel that you have become the word that you are repeating. Feel that your physical body, subtle body, all your nerves and your entire being are flooded with love or peace or light.

3 **Invite your friends.** Feel that you are standing at your heart's door and that you have invited love, peace, light, delight and all your other divine friends to visit you. But if complexity, insincerity, impurity, insecurity, doubt and other negative forces appear, please do not let them enter. Try to feel that both the divine qualities and the undivine qualities have taken the form of human beings, and that you can see them with your human eyes.

Every day try to invite one friend to enter your heart's door. This will be the beginning of a divine friendship. One day you will allow only your friend love to come in; the next day you will allow your friend joy to come in. After some time, you will have the capacity to invite more than one friend at a time. In the beginning you may not be able to pay attention to more than one friend at a time, but eventually you will be able to invite all your divine friends at once.

Q&A

Q I am looking for more joy in my life, but I don't feel confident about jumping into meditation to get it.

A When life is not giving you joy but you feel that you want joy, that means you are spiritually hungry. When you are spiritually hungry, you will eat spiritual food. When you are not hungry, you will not eat. For fifteen or twenty years you did not sincerely or intensely care for the spiritual life. Since you have not meditated for so many years, if you jump all at once into the sea of spirituality, you will not be able to swim. You cannot change your nature overnight. It has to be done slowly, steadily, gradually. First move around in the water, and gradually you will learn how to swim. Eventually there will come a time when you will be able to swim well. But since you have inner hunger, that means you are ready to start swimming.

No preparation, no attempt. No attempt, no progress. No progress, no perfection. No perfection, no satisfaction.

Mastering the Essentials

Mastering the Essentials

❧ Preparing Yourself to Meditate

When you meditate at home, you should have a corner of your room which is absolutely pure and sanctified—a sacred place which you use only for meditation. There you can make a shrine where you can keep a picture of your spiritual Master, or the Christ, or some other beloved spiritual figure whom you regard as your Master.

Before beginning to meditate, it is helpful if you can take a shower or proper bath. The cleanliness of the body is very helpful for the purification of the consciousness. If you are unable to take a shower or bath before sitting down to meditate, you should at least wash your face. It is also advisable to wear clean and light clothes.

It will also help if you burn incense and keep some fresh flowers on your shrine. When you smell the scent of incense, you get perhaps only an iota of inspiration and purification, but this iota can be added to your inner treasure. There are some people who say that it is not necessary to have flowers in front of you during meditation. They say, "The flower is inside; the thousand-petalled lotus is inside." But the physical flower on your shrine will remind you of the inner flower. Its colour, its fragrance and its pure consciousness will give you inspiration. From inspiration you get aspiration.

It is the same with using candles during meditation. The flame from a candle will not in itself give you aspiration, but when you see the outer flame immediately you feel that the flame of aspiration in your inner being is also climbing high, higher, highest. If someone is on the verge of God-realisation or has actually realised God, then these outer things will have no value. But if you know that your God-realisation is still a far cry, then they will definitely increase your aspiration.

When you are doing your individual daily meditation, try to meditate alone. This does not apply to husband and wife if they have the same spiritual Master; it is all right for them to meditate together. Otherwise, it is not advisable to meditate with others during your daily individual meditation. Collective meditation is also important, but for individual daily meditation it is better to meditate privately at one's own shrine.

> *Meditation is a divine gift. Meditation simplifies our outer life and energises our inner life. Meditation gives us a natural and spontaneous life, a life that becomes so natural and spontaneous that we cannot breathe without being conscious of our own divinity.*

Posture is important
When meditating, it is important to keep the spine straight and erect, and to keep the body relaxed. If the body is stiff, the divine and fulfilling qualities that are flowing in and through it during meditation will not be received. The body should not be uncomfortable, either. While you are meditating, your inner being will spontaneously take you to a comfortable position, and then it is up to you to maintain it. The main advantage of the lotus position is that it helps keep the spinal cord straight and erect. But it is not comfortable for most people. So the lotus position is not at all necessary for proper meditation. Many people meditate very well while seated in a chair.

Mastering the Essentials

Some people do physical exercises and postures. These exercises, called Hatha Yoga, relax the body and bring peace of mind for a short period. If someone is physically very restless and cannot stay still for more than a second, then these exercises will definitely help. But Hatha Yoga is not at all necessary. There are many aspirants who can just sit and make their minds calm and quiet without doing any Hatha Yoga.

It is not at all advisable to meditate while lying down, even for those who have been meditating for several years. Those who try to meditate while lying down will enter into the world of sleep or into a kind of inner drift or doze. Furthermore, while you are lying down, your breathing is not as satisfactory as it is when you are in a sitting position, since it is not conscious or controlled. Proper breathing is very important in meditation.

A soulful heart has discovered a supreme truth: to meditate on God is a privilege and not a duty.

Eyes open vs. eyes closed

People often ask me if they should meditate with their eyes open. In ninety out of one hundred cases, those who keep their eyes closed during meditation fall asleep. For five minutes they meditate, and then for fifteen minutes they remain in the world of sleep. There is no dynamic energy, but only lethargy, complacency and a kind of restful, sweet sensation.

When you keep your eyes closed during meditation and enter into the world of sleep, you may enjoy all kinds of fantasies. Your fertile imagination may make you feel that you are entering into the higher worlds. There are many ways you can make yourself believe that you are having a wonderful meditation. So it is best to meditate with the eyes half open and half closed. In this way you are the root of the tree and at the same time the topmost bough. The part of you that has the eyes half-open is the root, symbolising Mother-Earth. The part which has the eyes half-closed is the topmost branch, the world of vision or, let us say, Heaven. Your consciousness is on the highest level and it is also here on earth, trying to transform the world.

When you meditate with your eyes half open and half closed, you are doing what is called the "lion's meditation." Even while you are going deep within, you are focusing your conscious attention both on the physical plane and on the subconscious plane. Both the physical world, with its noise and distractions, and the subconscious world, the world of sleep, are inviting you, but you are conquering both of them. You are saying, "Look, I am alert. You cannot take me into your domain." Since your eyes are partly open, you will not fall asleep. So you are challenging the world of the subconscious. At the same time you are maintaining your mastery over the physical plane, because you can see what is going on around you.

How To

Breathing Exercises

1 **Breathing into the heart centre.** Please breathe in and hold your breath for a couple of seconds, and feel that you are holding the breath, which is life-energy, in your heart centre. This will help you to develop your inner meditation capacity.

2 **Becoming aware of the breath.** When you sit down to meditate, try to breathe in as slowly and quietly as possible, so that if somebody placed a tiny thread in front of your nose it would not move at all. And when you breathe out, try to breathe out even more slowly than you breathed in. If possible, leave a short pause between the end of your exhalation and the beginning of your inhalation. If you can, hold your breath for a few seconds. But if that is difficult, do not do it. Never do anything that will make you physically uncomfortable during meditation.

3 **Breathing in peace and joy.** The first thing that you have to think of when practising breathing techniques is purity. When you breathe in, if you can feel that the breath is coming directly from God, from Purity itself, then your breath can easily be purified. Then, each time you breathe in, try to feel that you are bringing infinite peace into your body. The opposite of peace is restlessness. When you breathe out, try to feel that you are expelling the restlessness within you and also the restlessness that you see all around you. When you breathe this way, you will find restlessness leaving you. After practising this a few times, please try to feel that you are breathing in power from the universe, and when you exhale, feel that all your fear is coming out of your body. After doing this a few times, try to feel that you are breathing in infinite joy and breathing out sorrow, suffering and melancholy.

4 **Cosmic energy.** Feel that you are breathing in not air but cosmic energy. Feel that tremendous cosmic energy is entering into you with each breath, and that you are going to use it to purify your body, vital, mind and heart. Feel that there is not a single place in your being that is not being occupied by the flow of cosmic energy. It is flowing like a river inside you, washing and purifying your entire being. Then, when you breathe out, feel that you are breathing out all the rubbish inside you—all your undivine thoughts, obscure ideas and impure actions. Anything inside your system that you call undivine, anything that you do not want to claim as your own, feel that you are exhaling.

This is not the traditional yogic *pranayama*, which is more complicated and systematised, but it is a most effective spiritual method of breathing. If you practise this method of breathing, you will soon see the results. In the beginning you will have to use your imagination, but after a while you will see and feel that it is not imagination at all but reality. You are consciously breathing in the energy which is flowing all around you, purifying yourself and emptying yourself of everything undivine. If you can breathe this way for five minutes every day, you will be able to make very fast progress. But it has to be done in a very conscious way, not mechanically.

5 **Total breathing.** When you reach a more advanced stage, you can try to feel that your breath is coming in and going out through every part of your body—through your heart, through your eyes, through your nose and even through your pores. Right now you can breathe only through your nose or your mouth, but a time will come when you will be able to breathe through every part of your body. Spiritual Masters can breathe even with their nose and mouth closed. When you have perfected this spiritual breathing, all your impurity and ignorance will be replaced by God's light, peace and power.

6 **One-four-two breathing.** As you breathe in, repeat once the name of God, the Christ or whomever you adore. Or, if your Master has given you a mantra, you can repeat that. This breath does not have to be long or deep. Then hold your breath and repeat the same name four times. And when you breathe out, repeat two times the name or mantra that you have chosen. You inhale for one count, hold your breath for four counts and exhale for two counts, inwardly repeating the sacred word. If you simply count the numbers—one-four-two—you do not get any vibration or inner feeling. But when you say the name of God, immediately God's divine qualities enter into you. Then, when you hold your breath, these divine qualities rotate inside you, entering into all your impurities, obscurities, imperfections and limitations. And when you breathe out, these same divine qualities carry away all your undivine, unprogressive and destructive qualities.

In the beginning you can start with a one-four-two count. When you become experienced in this breathing exercise, you will be able to do it to a count of four-sixteen-eight: breathing in for four counts, holding the breath for sixteen, and breathing out for eight. But this has to be done very gradually. Some people do an eight-thirty-two-sixteen count, but this is for the experts.

7 **Alternate breathing.** Another technique you can try is alternate breathing. This is done by pressing the right nostril closed with the thumb and taking in a long breath through the left nostril. As you breathe in, repeat God's name once. Then hold your breath for four counts repeating God's name four times. And finally release your right nostril, press your left nostril closed with your fourth finger and release your breath to the count of two—that is, two repetitions of God's name. Then do it the opposite way, starting with the left nostril pressed closed. In this system, when you breathe in, it does not have to be done quietly. Even if you make noise, no harm. But of course, these exercises should not be done in public or where other people are trying to meditate in silence.

You should not practise one-four-two breathing for more than four or five minutes, and you should not do alternate breathing more than a few times. If you do it twenty or forty or fifty times, heat will rise from the base of your spine and enter into your head, creating tension and a headache. It is like eating too much. Eating is good, but if you eat voraciously, it will upset your stomach. This inner heat acts the same way. If you draw it up beyond your capacity, then instead of giving you a peaceful mind, it will give you an arrogant, turbulent and destructive mind. Later, when you have developed your inner capacity, you can do this alternate breathing for ten or fifteen minutes.

Q Is it necessary to meditate only at home, or can we try to meditate wherever we are?

A Right now you are only a beginner. You can meditate at your best only when you are alone in your room or in the presence of your spiritual Master. If you try to meditate while driving or walking or sitting on the subway, you will not be able to go very deep. Again, it is not enough just to be seated before your shrine. While you are seated before your shrine, you have to feel an inner shrine within your heart; otherwise, you will not have a satisfactory meditation. Wherever you meditate, you must enter into your heart, where you can see and feel the living shrine of the Supreme. At your inner shrine you are safe and pro-

Mastering the Essentials

tected. You are guarded by the divine forces there. If you can meditate at this inner shrine, you are bound to make the fastest progress, because there you will meet with no opposition.

After you have meditated very sincerely for several years and developed some inner strength, at that time you will be able to meditate anywhere. Even if you are standing in the subway or walking along the street, you will not be disturbed. Eventually you have to learn how to do the highest meditation and, at the same time, be aware of what is happening in the outer world.

Q During meditation and prayer, some people concentrate on certain objects, like photographs or some other things. Is it wise for them to cling to these objects, or is it wiser for them to meditate on something that has no form, that they cannot see?

A When they meditate on something, they are not worshipping that particular thing as God. They are only receiving inspiration from that thing. I look at a candle and I see the flame, but I am not taking the flame as God. I am taking the flame as a source of inspiration. This flame inspires me and increases my aspiration to climb upward with a burning inner cry. I may keep a flower before me when I meditate. The flower is not God, although inside the flower is God. But the flower inspires me and offers me purity. I may burn incense. Incense itself is not God for me, but incense gives me a feeling of purity, and helps me in my spiritual progress.

Anything that inspires me I shall use in order to increase my aspiration, whether it is a picture, a candle or a flower. For when my inspiration and aspiration increase, I feel that I have taken one step more toward my goal. But the candle or the picture or the flower itself is not the object of my adoration.

Q Eventually, when we realise God, will all these things drop off?

A When we become expert in our aspiration-life, then no outer form will remain. We will become one with the Formless. But in the beginning, it is necessary to approach God through form. In the beginning, a child reads aloud. He has to convince his parents, he has to convince himself, that he is reading the words. If he does not read aloud, he feels that he is not reading at all. But when the child becomes adept, he reads in silence. By then, he and his parents know that he can really read, so the outer form can drop away. But these outer forms are of paramount importance during the seeker's preliminary stages. Eventually they will go, when they are no longer necessary.

Q Is it all right to meditate after eating, or is fasting desirable?

A It is not good to meditate just after eating a large meal. The body has thousands of subtle spiritual nerves. These nerves become heavy after a big meal and will not permit you to have the highest type of meditation. The body will be heavy, the consciousness will be heavy, the nerves will be heavy, and your meditation will not be good. When you meditate properly, you feel that your whole existence, like a bird, is flying high, higher, highest. But when your consciousness is heavy, you cannot go up.

So it is always advisable to meditate on an empty stomach. At least two hours should elapse between your meal and the time that you sit down to meditate. But again, if you are really pinched with hunger when you go to meditate, your meditation will not be satisfactory. Your hunger, like a monkey, will constantly bother you. In that case, it is advisable to have just a glass of milk or juice before meditating. This will not ruin your meditation.

But to refrain from eating a large meal before meditation is not the same as fasting. Fasting is not at all necessary for meditation. By fasting you can purify yourself to some extent. Once a month, if you wish, you can fast for a day to purify your existence of outer aggressions and greed. But by fasting frequently, you approach death rather than God. Fasting is not the answer for self-purification. The answer is constant, soulful meditation, unreserved love for God and unconditional surrender to God.

Q Is it necessary to be a vegetarian in order to follow the spiritual life?

A The vegetarian diet does play a role in the spiritual life. Purity is of paramount importance for an aspirant. This purity we must establish in the body, in the vital and in the mind. When we eat meat, the aggressive animal consciousness enters into us. Our nerves become agitated and restless, and this can interfere with our meditation. If a seeker does not stop eating meat, generally he does not get subtle experiences or subtle visions.

At one time the animal consciousness was necessary for forward movement. Animals are by nature aggressive but, at the same time, there is some dynamic push forward in the animal consciousness. If we had not had animal qualities, we would have remained inert, like trees, or we would have remained in the stone consciousness where there is no growth or movement. But unfortunately the animal consciousness also contains many unillumined and destructive qualities. Now we have entered into the spiritual life, so the role of the animal consciousness is no longer necessary in our life.

From the animal consciousness we have entered into the human consciousness, and now we are trying to enter into the divine consciousness.

The mild qualities of fruits and vegetables help us to establish, in our inner life as well as in our outer life, the qualities of sweetness, softness, simplicity and purity. If we are vegetarians, this helps our inner being to strengthen its own existence. Inwardly, we are praying and meditating; outwardly, the food we are taking from Mother-Earth is helping us too, giving us not only energy but also aspiration.

Some people feel that it is meat that gives them strength. But if they go deep within, they may discover that it is their own idea about meat that is giving them strength. One can change that idea and feel that it is not meat but the spiritual energy pervading one's body that gives one strength. That energy comes from meditation as well as from proper nourishment. The strength that one can get from aspiration and meditation is infinitely more powerful than the strength one can get from meat.

Many spiritual seekers have come to the conclusion that a vegetarian is in a position to make quicker progress in the spiritual life. But along with a vegetarian diet, one must pray and meditate. If one has aspiration, the vegetarian diet will help considerably; the body's purity will help one's inner aspiration to become more intense and more soulful. But again, if one is not a vegetarian, that does not mean that one will not make spiritual progress or will not be able to realise God.

Mastering the Essentials

Sometimes I must be silent,
For that is the only way
To know a little better,
To think a little wiser,
To become a little more perfect,
To claim God a little sooner.

The Silent Mind

The Silent Mind

❦ Quieting the Mind

No matter which path you follow for meditation, the first and foremost task is to try to make the mind calm and quiet. If the mind is constantly roaming, if it is all the time a victim of merciless thoughts, then you will make no progress whatsoever. The mind has to be made calm and quiet so that when the light descends from above, you can be fully conscious of it. In your conscious observation and conscious acceptance of light, you will enter into a profound meditation and see the purification, transformation and illumination of your life.

How will you make the mind calm and quiet? The mind has its own power, and right now this power is stronger than your present eagerness and determination to meditate. But if you can get help from your heart, then gradually you will be able to control your mind. The heart, in turn, gets constant assistance from the soul, which is all light and all power.

Emptying the mind

You must not think that when there is nothing in your mind, you will become a fool or act like an idiot. This is not true. If you can keep your mind calm and quiet for ten or fifteen minutes, a new world will dawn within you. This is the root of all spiritual progress. Right now you can make your mind calm and quiet for only a few seconds, or for a minute, but if you can maintain your calmness, poise and tranquillity for half an hour or even for fifteen minutes, I assure you that inside your tranquillity a new world with tremendous divine light and power will grow.

When you do not have any thought in your mind, please do not feel that you are totally lost. On the contrary, feel that something divine is being prepared in your pure and aspiring nature. You cannot expect immediate results. The farmer sows the seed and then he waits; he never expects the crop to spring forth all at once. It takes a few weeks or a few months to germinate. Your mind can be like a fertile field. If you plant the seed of silence and poise and cultivate it patiently, sooner or later you are bound to reap the bumper crop of illumination.

The mind is not necessary for meditation, because thinking and meditating are absolutely different things. When we meditate, we do not think at all. The aim of meditation is to free ourselves from all thought. Thought is like a dot on a blackboard. Whether it is good or bad, it is there. Only if there is no thought whatsoever can we grow into the highest reality. Even in profound meditation thoughts can come in, but not in the highest, deepest meditation. In the highest meditation, there will be only light.

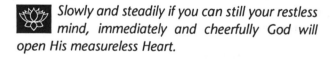 *Slowly and steadily if you can still your restless mind, immediately and cheerfully God will open His measureless Heart.*

Beyond the mind

In light, vision and reality are one. You are sitting there and I am standing here. Let us say that I am the vision and you are the reality. I have to look at you and enter into you in order to know you. But in the highest meditation reality and vision are one. Where you are, I also am there; where I am, you are. We are one. That is why in the highest meditation we do not need thoughts. In the highest meditation the knower and the thing to be known are one.

Even reflection, which is a quiet kind of introspective thinking, is far from the disciplined vastness of meditation. The moment we start thinking, we play with limitation and bondage. Our thoughts, no matter how sweet or delicious at the moment, are painful and destructive in the long run because they limit and bind us. In the thinking mind there is no reality. Each moment we are building a world, and the following moment we are breaking it. The mind has its purpose, but in the spiritual life we have to go far above the mind to where there is eternal peace, eternal wisdom and eternal light. When we go beyond thinking with the help of our aspiration and meditation, only then can we see and enjoy God's Reality and God's Vision together.

How To

Purifying the Mind

The mind is almost always impure, and it almost always brings in unaspiring thoughts. Even when it is not doing this, the mind is still a victim to doubt, jealousy, hypocrisy, fear and other undivine qualities. All negative things first attack the mind. The mind may reject them for a minute, but again they knock at the mind's door. This is the nature of the mind. The heart is much, much purer. Affection, love, devotion, surrender and other divine qualities are already there in the heart. That is why the heart is much purer than the mind. Even if you have fear or jealousy in the heart, the good qualities of the heart will still come forward.

But again, the heart may not be totally pure because the vital being is near the heart. The lower vital, which is situated near the navel, tends to come up and touch the heart centre. It makes the heart impure by its influence and proximity. But at least the heart is not like the mind, which deliberately opens its door to impure ideas. The heart is far better than the mind. And best is the soul. The soul is all purity, light, bliss and divinity.

1 **Becoming the soul.** In order to purify your mind, the best thing to do is to feel every day for a few minutes during your meditation that you have no mind. Say to yourself, "I have no mind, I have no mind. What I have is the heart." Then after some time feel, "I don't have a heart. What I have is the soul." When you say, "I have the soul," at that time you will be flooded with purity. But again you have to go deeper and farther by saying not only, "I have the soul," but also "I am the soul." At that time, imagine the most beautiful child you have ever seen, and feel that your soul is infinitely more beautiful than that child.

The moment you can say and feel, "I *am* the soul," and meditate on this truth, your soul's infinite purity will enter into your heart. Then, from the heart, the infinite purity will enter into your mind. When you can truly feel that you are only the soul, the soul will purify your mind.

2 **The inner flame.** Before you meditate, try to imagine a flame inside your heart. Right now the flame may be tiny and flickering; it may not be a powerful flame. But one day it will definitely become most powerful and most illumining. Try to imagine that this flame is illumining your mind. In the beginning you may not be able to concentrate according to your satisfaction because the mind is not focused. The mind is constantly thinking of many things. It has become a victim of many uncomely thoughts. The mind does not have proper illumination, so imagine a beautiful flame inside your heart, illumining you. Bring that illumining flame inside your mind. Then you will gradually see a streak of light inside your mind. When your mind starts getting illumined, it will be very, very easy to concentrate for a long time, and also to concentrate more deeply.

3 **Purifying the breath.** Before you start your meditation, repeat "Supreme" about twenty times as fast as possible in order to purify your breath. Feel that you are really growing into the very Breath of God. Unless and until the breath is purified, the mind will not remain one-pointed.

4 **God wants me, I need God.** Focus your attention on a picture. You can look at your Master's picture or you can look at yourself in the mirror. If you concentrate on your own reflection, feel that you are totally one with the physical being that you are seeing. Then try to enter into the image that you are seeing. From there you should try to grow with one thought: God wants you and you need God. Repeat: "God wants me, I need God. God wants me, I need God." Then you will see that slowly, steadily and unerringly this divine thought is entering into you and permeating your inner and outer existence, giving you purity in your mind, vital and body.

5 **Asserting control over the mind.** You can tell your mind, "I shall not allow you to go in your own way. Now I want to think of God." Repeat the name of God inwardly or aloud. Then say, "I want to have purity in my whole existence." Then repeat "purity, purity, purity." At that time you are not allowing your mind to think of impurity or of any other thing. Don't give your mind a chance to wander; simply utilise your mind for your own purpose. You have millions of things to accomplish in and through the mind. But the mind is so naughty and mischievous that if you don't utilise it, it will utilise you.

6 **Throw them out.** Each time an undivine thought enters into your mind, throw it out of your mind. It is like a foreign element, a thief, that has entered your room. Why should you consciously allow a thief to remain in your room when you have the capacity to throw him out? When an undivine thought enters into your mind, just capture the thought and throw it into the blazing fire of your inner aspiration.

7 **Strangling bad thoughts.** When a thought comes that is not pure, good or divine, immediately repeat the word "Supreme" very fast. The Supreme is my Guru, your Guru, everybody's Guru. Repeat "Supreme" very fast, and each time you use the word "Supreme," feel that you are creating a snake that will coil around the undivine thought and strangle it.

Q I am a beginner in meditation, and I find that I cannot control my thoughts. How can I have a successful meditation?

A If you are a beginner, try to allow only divine thoughts to enter into you, and not undivine thoughts. It is better not to have any thoughts at all during meditation, but it is next to impossible for the beginner to have a mind without thoughts. So you can begin by having good thoughts: "I want to be good, I want to be more spiritual, I want to love God more, I want to exist only for Him." Let these ideas grow within you. Start with one or two divine ideas: "Today I will be absolutely pure. I will not allow any bad thought, but only peace, to enter into me." When you allow one divine thought to grow inside you, you will see that immediately your consciousness changes for the better.

Start with divine ideas: "Today I want to feel that I am really a child of God." This will not be a mere feeling but an actual reality. Feel that the Virgin Mary is holding the child Christ. Feel that the Divine Mother is holding you in her arms like a baby. Then feel: "I really want to have wisdom-light. I want to walk with my Father. Wherever He goes I will go with Him. I will get light from Him."

Some people don't have ideas like this. Creative thoughts and ideas don't come. There is just a vacuum. You may ask which is better—to have many silly messages in the mind or no messages at all. But there is a negative, inconscient way of meditating which has no life in it. This is not the silent mind. It is not productive. In real meditation, the mind is silent but at the same time it is conscious.

Q Ideally, should one reject all thoughts during meditation?

A The best thing is to try not to allow any thought to enter into your mind, whether it is a good thought or a bad thought. It is as though you are in your room, and somebody is knocking at your door. You have no idea whether it is an enemy or a friend. Divine thoughts are your true friends, and undivine thoughts are your enemies. You would like to allow your friends to enter, but you do not know who your friends are. And even if you *do* know who your friends are, when you open the door for them you may find that your enemies are also there.

Then, before your friends can cross the threshold, your enemies will also enter. You may not even notice any undivine thoughts, but while the divine thoughts are entering, the undivine thoughts, like thieves, will also secretly enter and create tremendous confusion. Once they have entered, it is very difficult to chase them out. For that you need the strength of solid spiritual discipline. For fifteen minutes you may cherish spiritual thoughts and then, in just a fleeting second, an undivine thought will come. So the best thing is not to allow any thoughts at all during your meditation. Just keep the door bolted from inside.

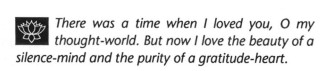 *There was a time when I loved you, O my thought-world. But now I love the beauty of a silence-mind and the purity of a gratitude-heart.*

Your real friends will not go away. They will think, "Something is wrong with him. Usually he is so kind to us. So there must be some special reason why he is not opening the door." They have sympathetic oneness, so they will wait indefinitely. But your enemies will wait just for a few minutes. Then they will lose all patience and say, "It is beneath our dignity to waste our time here." These enemies have their pride. They will say, "Who cares? Who needs him? Let us go and attack somebody else." If you pay no attention to a monkey, the monkey will eventually go away and bite somebody else. But your friends will say, "No, we need him

The Silent Mind

and he needs us. We will wait indefinitely for him." So after a few minutes your enemies will go away. Then you can open the door and your dearest friends will be there waiting for you.

If you meditate regularly and devotedly, after some time you will become inwardly strong. Then you will be able to welcome the divine thoughts and chase away the undivine thoughts. If you are getting a thought of divine love, divine peace or divine power, then you will allow that thought to enter into you and expand. You will let it play and grow in the garden of your mind. While the thought is playing and you are playing with it, you will see that you are growing into it. Each divine thought that you let in will create a new and fulfilling world for you, and will surcharge your entire being with divinity.

After a few years of meditation you will have enough inner strength to let in even the undivine thoughts. When an undivine thought comes into your mind, you will not reject it; you will transform it. When somebody undivine knocks at your door, if you have enough strength to compel him to behave properly once he enters, then you can open the door for him. Eventually you have to accept the challenge and conquer these wrong thoughts; otherwise, they will come back to bother you again and again.

I am so proud of my mind. Why? Because it has started enjoying little things: a simple thought, a pure heart, a humble life.

You have to be a divine potter. If the potter is afraid to touch the clay, then the clay will remain always clay and the potter will not be able to offer anything to the world. But if the potter is not afraid, he can transform the clay into something beautiful and useful. It is your bounden duty to transform undivine thoughts, but only when you are in a position to do so safely.

Q What is the best way to deal with undivine thoughts that come during meditation?

A The moment a negative or unaspiring thought enters your mind, you should try to use your aspiration to reject it, because during meditation everything is very intense. While you are talking or engaging in ordinary activities, you can have any kind of thought, for your thoughts are not intense at those times. But if any undivine thought comes during meditation, the power of your meditation enlarges and intensifies it. Your spiritual life grows weaker the moment you allow your mind to indulge in unaspiring thoughts during meditation. If a good thought comes, you can try to enlarge it, or you can try to lift it up to a higher level. But if you have a bad thought, try to cut it off immediately.

How will you do this? If the thought that is attacking you is coming from the outer world, try to muster your soul's will from your heart and bring it right in front of your forehead. The moment your soul's will is seen by the thought which is trying to enter into you, that thought is bound to disappear.

But if you do not have the inner capacity to do this, do not become upset. Sometimes when wrong thoughts come during meditation, the seeker feels that the strength of the wrong thought is so powerful that even if he has meditated for two or three hours, it is all useless. One ordinary thought or wrong thought comes in and he feels that he has lost everything. This is foolish. As long as you do not allow your mind to dwell on them, you should not give any importance to wrong thoughts at that particular moment.

If emotional thoughts, lower vital thoughts or sex thoughts enter into you during meditation, and you are not able to keep them out or throw them out, try to feel that these thoughts are as insignificant as ants. Just pay no attention to them. If you can feel that the spiritual power that you have received from your meditation is infinitely stronger than the power of the wrong thoughts, then these wrong thoughts cannot utilise your meditative power for their own purpose. But what often happens is that you become terribly afraid of these thoughts and dwell on them. By thinking about them and being afraid of them, you give them power.

It is true that wrong thoughts can become intense during meditation. But you can easily bring to the fore good thoughts that are infinitely more powerful. During meditation when wrong thoughts come to you, immediately try to recollect one of your sweetest or highest divine experiences. Enter into your own experience which you had a few days ago or a few years ago, and try to bring it into your mental consciousness. You will see that while you are fully immersed in your own experience, the thought from the lower vital plane is bound to leave you because the highest, deepest, purest joy is in your consciousness. Divine joy is infinitely more powerful than pleasure. The nectar-delight of your own spiritual experience is infinitely stronger than your lower vital forces. In this way you can solve the problem without leaving your meditation.

Wrong thoughts come to attack you and take away your divine feelings, divine thoughts and divine power. But when you pay all attention to divine thoughts and encourage and cherish only divine feelings, in many cases the wrong thoughts just go away. They say, "He does not care for us. We have no place here." Wrong thoughts also have their pride, and they are terribly jealous of divine thoughts. They do not care for you if you do not care for them.

So far I have been talking about thoughts that come from outside. But sometimes undivine thoughts arise from within. In the beginning it is difficult to distinguish between thoughts that are coming from outside and those that come from within. But gradually you will be able to feel the difference. The thoughts that are coming from outside can be driven back faster than the thoughts that attack you from within. But if impure and unlit thoughts arise from inside you, then you can do one of two things. You can try to feel that there is a hole right at the top of your head. Then make the thoughts flow out like a river which goes only in one direction and does not come back. They are then gone, and you are freed from them. The other method is to feel that you are the boundless ocean, all calm and quiet, and that the thoughts are like fish on the surface. The ocean pays no attention to the ripples of the fish.

Q Why is it that I am constantly bothered by thoughts?

A You are constantly bothered by thoughts because you are trying to meditate inside your mind. The very nature of the mind is to welcome thoughts—good thoughts, bad thoughts, divine thoughts, undivine thoughts. If you want to control the mind with your human will, then it will be like asking a monkey or a fly not to bother you. The very nature of a monkey is to bite and pinch; the very nature of a fly is to bother people.

The mind needs a superior power to keep it quiet. This superior power is the power of the soul. You have to bring to the fore the light of the soul from inside your heart. You are the possessor of two rooms: the heart-room and the mind-room. Right now the mind-room is obscure, unlit and impure; it is unwilling to open to the light. But the heart-room is always open to the light, for that is where the soul abides. Instead of concentrating on the mind, if you can concentrate and meditate on the reality that is inside the heart, then this reality will come forward.

If you stay in the mind-room all the time with the hope of illumining it from within, you will waste your time. If I want to light a candle, I must use a flame that is already burning, already illumined. The heart-room, fortunately, is already illumined. Once you are well-established in the heart, when you are surcharged with the soul's light, at that time you can enter into the mind-room to illumine the mind. But first you have to bring to the fore the soul's light, which is available most powerfully in the heart. The light of the soul will not torture or punish the mind. On the contrary, it will act like a most affectionate mother who feels that the imperfections of her child are her own imperfections. The heart will offer its light to the mind in order to transform the nature of the mind.

Q I try to keep my mind from wandering during meditation, but I have very little success.

A You are not exercising the capacity of your heart; you are only exercising the mind's power. Very often when I am concentrating on you, I see that your mind is rotating like a wheel. When the mind rotates, it is very difficult for the Supreme to act in your mind. But when your heart aspires even for a second, the Supreme opens the door and enters.

From now on, please try to feel that you do not have a mind at all. This does not mean that you will be like a brute or an animal. No! The human mind is not necessary because you have a superior instrument called the heart. If you can stay in your heart for five minutes, even if you do not pray or meditate, your consciousness will be raised.

The heart is like a fountain of peace, joy and love. You can sit at the base of the fountain and just enjoy. There is no need to pray to the Supreme to give you this or that, for you will get all the things that you want—and infinitely more—from this fountain. But you will get them in the Supreme's own way. If you can please the Supreme by staying always in the presence of your heart-fountain, your desires will be fulfilled most luminously. They may be the same desires that you have always had, but they will be touched on a very high level with luminosity. Before He fulfils these, the Supreme will transform each desire into aspiration with His light.

Q During a meditation, if there is a noise or disturbance, is it better to include it in the meditation or try to shut it out and pursue the meditation?

A Each seeker has to know his own standard of meditation. If you are a beginner, you should feel that anything that is not part of the meditation is like an intruder, and you should not allow an intruder to enter and disturb you. But if you are very advanced, and there is a disturbing sound or noise during your meditation, you can go deep into the sound itself and try to assimilate it. If you have the capacity, then in your own consciousness you can transform the attack of a powerful and challenging foreign element into an inner music, which will add to your meditation.

Q If I get creative ideas while I am meditating, should I follow them or should I just try to feel with my heart?

A As soon as you get a positive idea, you should consider it as a blessing from the Supreme. But you have to know what kind of inspiration it is. If it is

The Silent Mind

an illumining inspiration, then you should follow it. If it is a creative inspiration to do something really good, then follow it. Any creative thought, anything that gives you a higher goal, should be followed. If a particular inspiration brings something new into your life and is able to transform your life, then that inspiration you should follow.

You may feel that inspiration is only in the mind whereas aspiration is only in the heart. But aspiration can be in the mind and inspiration can be in the heart. Inspiration can come to aspiration and vice versa. But inspiration must be of a very high type. Otherwise it cannot help you in your meditation at all. During meditation if you are inspired to make most delicious cookies, this kind of inspiration is a waste of time.

If it is an illumining inspiration, then please take these creative ideas as your own progress. When you get creative ideas, you have to know that they are creations from another world which want to manifest on the physical plane. When your meditation is over, you should write down the ideas. Afterwards you can elaborate on them.

Q Is it bad to expect some particular thing when we meditate?

A During your meditation just try to throw your inner and outer existence into the Supreme. You do not have to think of anything; just throw yourself into the sea of light, peace, bliss and power. But do not expect any particular divine quality or result, because then you are binding yourself and binding God. That is because human expectation is very limited. When you expect, immediately the mind acts, and then your receptivity becomes very limited. But if you do not expect, then the problem of receptivity becomes God's problem. At that time He is bound to give you everything in boundless measure, and at the same time to create the receptivity in you to receive what He has to offer.

The highest type of meditation is done in silence, with one objective: to please God in His own way. When you meditate, if you can feel that you are pleasing God in God's own way, then that is the best type of meditation. Otherwise, if you start meditating in order to get joy, you will get joy; but you will not get boundless joy, precisely because you have not pleased your Eternal Beloved, God, in His own way. What the Saviour Christ said is absolutely the highest truth: "Let Thy Will be done." Before you meditate, if you can offer the result of your meditation to the Source and say, "I wish to become Your perfect instrument so You can fulfil Yourself in and through me in Your own way," this is the highest, absolutely the highest, type of meditation.

Your mind has a flood of questions. There is but one teacher who can answer them. Who is the teacher? Your silence-loving heart.

Do you want to be happy? Then do not overestimate the power of your mind and do not under-estimate the light of your heart.

Your Spiritual Heart:
The Home of Peace

Your Spiritual Heart: The Home of Peace

❦ Discovering Your Treasure Within

It is better to meditate in the heart than in the mind. The mind is like Times Square on New Year's Eve; the heart is like a lonely cave in the Himalayas. If you meditate in the mind, you will be able to meditate for perhaps five minutes; and out of that five minutes, for one minute you may meditate powerfully. After that you will feel your whole head getting tense. First you get joy and satisfaction; then you may feel a barren desert. But if you meditate in the heart, you acquire the capacity to identify yourself with the joy and satisfaction that you get, and then it becomes permanently yours.

If you meditate in the mind, you do not identify; you try to enter into something. When you want to enter into somebody else's house to get what that person has, either you have to break down the door or you have to plead with the owner of the house to open the door. When you plead, you feel that you are a stranger, and the owner of the house also feels that you are a stranger. Then he thinks, "Why should I allow a stranger to come into my house?" But if you use the heart, immediately the heart's qualities of softness, sweetness, love and purity come to the fore. When the owner of the house sees that you are all heart, immediately his own heart will become one with yours and he will let you in. He will feel your oneness with him and say, "What do you want from my house? If you need peace, then take it. If you need light, then take it."

One more thing: if you enter into the house with your mind, you will see some delicious fruit and immediately try to grab it. You are satisfied when you get it, even though you do not have the capacity to eat all the fruit. But if you use the heart, you will find that your capacity of receptivity is boundless. Again, if you use the mind, you will try to make a selection. You will say, "This piece of fruit is better; this one is worse." But if you enter into the house with your heart, you will feel that everything there is yours, and you will enjoy it all. The heart centre is the centre of oneness. First you identify with the truth and then, on the strength of your identification, you become the truth.

 Remain always in the sunshine of your heart until its illumining rays ha ° also flooded your mind.

Heart and soul

If you meditate in the heart, you are meditating where the soul is. True, the light and consciousness of the soul permeate the whole body, but there is a specific place where the soul resides most of the time, and that is in the heart. If you want illumination, you have to get it from the soul, which is inside the heart. When you know what you want and where to find it, the sensible thing is to go to that place. Otherwise, it is like going to the hardware store to get groceries.

There is a vast difference between what you can get from the mind and what you can get from the heart. The mind is limited; the heart is unlimited. Deep within you are infinite peace, light and bliss. To get a limited quantity is an easy task. Meditation in the mind can give it to you. But you can get infinitely more if you meditate in the heart. Suppose you have the opportunity to work at two places. At one place you will earn two hundred dollars and at the other place five hundred dollars. If you are wise, you will not waste your time at the first place.

As long as you have tremendous faith in the mind, which complicates and confuses everything, you will be doomed to disappointment in your meditation. Ordinary people think that complication is wisdom. But spiritual people know that God is very simple. It is in simplicity, not in complexity, that the real truth abides.

I am not saying that the mind is always bad. No, it need not be. But the mind is limited. At most, what you can get from the mind is inspiration, which itself is limited. For real aspiration you have to go to the heart. Aspiration comes from the heart because the illumination of the soul is always there. When you meditate on the heart, not only do you get aspiration, but you also get the fulfilment of that aspiration: the soul's infinite peace, light and bliss.

Q I would like to know how one can reach the spiritual heart during meditation.

A The spiritual heart is located right in the centre of the chest. You can feel the spiritual heart when you are aspiring intensely, and you can also see it with the third eye. If you find it difficult to meditate on the spiritual heart, you can concentrate on the physical heart in the chest. But after you meditate there for a few months or for a year, you will feel that inside the ordinary human heart is the divine heart, and inside the divine heart is the soul. When you feel this, you will start meditating on the spiritual heart.

To reach the spiritual heart you have to feel that you do not have a mind, you do not have arms, you do not have legs, you have only the heart. Then you have to feel that you do not *have* the heart, but that you *are* the heart. When you can feel that you are the heart and nothing else, then easily you will be able to reach your spiritual heart during your meditation.

Q I find it very difficult to leave the mind and enter into the heart. What should I do?

A Just throw the mind and all its possessions into the heart. You may think, "If I throw away my mind, then how can I exist? I will become an idiot." But I tell you, the mind that you use to converse with people, the mind that you use to acquire information, the mind that you use for ordinary earthly activities, cannot take you even an inch toward God-realisation. It is lame. It is blind. It is deaf.

Try to feel that your whole existence, from the soles of your feet to the crown of your head, is the soul. Soulfully repeat, "I am the soul, I am the soul." If you can soulfully repeat this for five minutes, then the resistance of the physical mind will go away and only the soul will exist for you. Once you live in the soul and bring the soul's light forward, then this light will bring the physical mind to the higher regions or it will bring down peace from above. In either case, the physical mind as you know it will be transformed, and you will not have any more problems.

Q When I am meditating sometimes I have trouble distinguishing whether I really feel my heart or whether it is my mind that I am experiencing.

A If it is really your heart, then you will get a sense of pure satisfaction. If it is the mind, you may get satisfaction, but immediately you will also get doubt. Your experience will be attacked by other thoughts: "I am so bad, so impure, so ignorant. This morning I told a lie and yesterday I did something else that was bad, so how can I have this kind of satisfaction?" When that kind of idea comes, you will know that your experience was from the mind.

When you get an experience from the mind, you may temporarily feel very happy. But the joy will not remain, because you will not be able to establish your identification with what the mind has seen or felt or realised. But once you get an experience from the heart, immediately you will feel your oneness with it, and your joy will be lasting.

When you see a flower with your mind, you appreciate and admire it. But when you see it with your heart, immediately you feel that your heart is inside the flower or that the flower is inside your heart. So when you have an experience, if you are one with the experience itself, then you will know it is from the heart. But if you feel that the experience is something that you are achieving outside yourself, then it is from the mind.

Q What is the difference between going high and going deep in meditation?

A There is a great difference in the methods of meditation, although ultimately height and depth become one. When we want to go deep in meditation, we have to start our journey from the spiritual heart. We should feel that we are digging or travelling very deep into our heart. We are travelling inward, not backward or downward towards the feet. Below the knees the plane of inconscience starts. If we feel that we are going downward, then it is not spiritual depth we are getting but only the lower planes of consciousness. The spiritual heart is infinitely vast, so there is no limit to how deep we can go. We can never touch its boundaries, because the spiritual heart embodies the vast universe that we see, and at the same time it is larger and vaster than the universe.

When we want to go high in meditation, then we have to feel an upward direction in our meditation. Our aspiration is climbing, climbing fearlessly toward the Highest. We must pass through the thousand-petalled lotus at the top of the head. Again, the distance is infinitely vast. There is no end to our upward journey because we are travelling in Infinity. We are climbing toward the ever-transcending Beyond. In terms of distance, upward and inward are both infinite journeys toward one Goal, the Supreme.

We cannot go high by using the mind, however. We must pass through the mind, beyond the mind, and into the realm of the spiritual heart. The domain of the spiritual heart is infinitely higher and vaster than that of the highest mind. Far beyond the mind is the domain of the heart. The heart is boundless in every direction, so inside the heart is the highest height as well as the deepest depth.

The higher we can go, the deeper we can go. Again, the deeper we can go, the higher we can go. It works simultaneously. If we can meditate very powerfully, then we are bound to feel that we are going both very high and very deep. Height and depth go together, but they work in two different dimensions, so to speak. But if a person can go very high in his meditation, then he also has the capacity to go very deep.

Before we realise the Highest, we feel that there is a difference between height and depth. When we are climbing up we feel that we have reached a certain height, and when we are diving deep within, we feel that we have reached a certain depth. But height and depth are all in the mental consciousness. Once we go beyond the barrier of the mind and enter into the Universal Consciousness, we see everything as one and inseparable. At that time Reality is singing and dancing within us, and we become the Reality itself. It has no height, no depth, no length. It is all one and at the same time it is always transcending itself.

Q What will happen if I meditate on the navel centre?

A At this point in your spiritual development, it is not a good idea for you to meditate on the navel centre. This is the centre of dynamism, strength and power. If you misuse this dynamism, it becomes brutal aggression. The navel centre is also the emotional centre. With this emotion you can expand yourself and become the Infinite. But instead, if you do not have abundant purity in your nature, you will become a victim to earthly pleasure-life. You should meditate on the heart centre to get peace, love and joy. When you have these qualities, you will feel that peace itself is power, love itself is power, joy itself is power.

Q What is the relationship between the third eye and the heart centre?

A Let us say that the heart is consciousness and the third eye is light, although there is no actual difference between the two things. The third eye has infinite light and at the same time it is infinite light. The spiritual heart possesses infinite consciousness and at the same time it is infinite consciousness. But infinite light and infinite consciousness are one and the same. This moment the infinite light—which I am calling the third eye—is a building, and inside it the heart resides. But the next moment the infinite consciousness—

which I am calling the heart—can become the building, and the third eye will become the resident. They constantly change, because they are not really separate. Sometimes we see light before consciousness, while other times we see consciousness before light. The one which we see first, we feel is the source of the other. But a time comes when we see that light and consciousness are inseparable.

The heart usually embodies sweetness and love, and the third eye embodies power and illumination. But those who are very wise will feel that the third eye is also the heart, for what else is the heart except that which gives us satisfaction? And what gives us satisfaction? Only light! So if light from the third eye gives us satisfaction, then naturally we are dealing with the heart's quality. And what gives us the highest wisdom? Wisdom comes only when we go deep inside the inmost recesses of our heart, where Infinity, Eternity and Immortality play. To possess Infinity as our very own, to possess infinite light and bliss eternally as our very own, is real wisdom. So we can say that wisdom comes from the heart.

Q Is it desirable to try to open the third eye in meditation?

A The inner eye should be opened only when there is inner purity and maturity, and when neither the past nor the future will disturb you. Many times the vessel is not ready, but by means of tremendous determination a seeker does succeed in opening the third eye. Then the result is most discouraging and damaging. When you are not spiritually mature, if you see with your third eye that your mother is going to die tomorrow, then you will die today with worry and anxiety. Or if you become aware of some unfortunate incident that took place in your past, you will feel extremely miserable and you will not have the strength to continue going forward.

There are people who have opened the centre between the eyebrows before having opened their heart centre and, by the Grace of the Supreme, have not made serious mistakes in using this power. But most of the time, unless and until the heart centre is opened and the emotional part of one's nature is totally purified, the seeker will fall victim to merciless temptation if he opens the third eye. He will try to see something inwardly and immediately he will tell others, or he will try to enter into somebody out of curiosity to see what is happening in that person's nature. There are a thousand and one things which can eventually lead the seeker far, far away from the path of spirituality.

For beginners especially, it is always advisable to meditate on the heart centre. In fact, even if you are advanced, you should meditate there, because in the heart centre you get joy and become part and parcel of whatever you are meditating on. If you concentrate on the third eye, you may not have the feeling of oneness. You may see light, but you will feel that it is not yours; you will think that perhaps it was not light at all but just imagination or hallucination. Doubt may enter into your mind. But when you use the heart, the joy that you get you immediately feel is yours; the peace that you feel is yours; anything that you feel becomes yours. This is the heart's capacity for oneness.

O my heart, O heart of mine, you are my lifeboat. You sail the uncharted seas of ignorance and reach the Golden Shore of the Beyond. O sweet, sweeter, sweetest heart of mine, you are not only God's. God also is yours.

We concentrate because we want to reach the Goal. We meditate because we want to live in the heart of the Goal. We contemplate because we want to become the Goal.

Concentration, Meditation & Contemplation:

Three Steps to Self-Fulfilment

Chapter 6
Concentration, Meditation & Contemplation: Three Steps to Self-Fulfilment

❦ The Arrow and the Bow

Concentration is the arrow. Meditation is the bow.

When we concentrate, we focus all our energies upon some subject or object in order to unveil its mysteries. When we meditate, we rise from our limited consciousness into a higher consciousness where the vastness of silence reigns supreme.

Concentration wants to seize the knowledge it aims at. Meditation wants to identify itself with the knowledge it seeks.

Concentration does not allow disturbance, the thief, to enter into its armory. Meditation lets him in. Why? Just to catch the thief red-handed.

Concentration is the commander who orders the dispersed consciousness to come to attention.

Concentration and absolute firmness are not only inseparable but also interdependent divine warriors.

Concentration challenges the enemy to a duel and fights him. Meditation, with its silent smile, diminishes the challenge of the enemy.

Concentration says to God: "Father, I am coming to You." Meditation says to God: "Father, do come to me."

An aspirant has two genuine teachers: concentration and meditation. Concentration is always strict with the student; meditation is strict at times. But both of them are solemnly interested in their student's progress.

The Power of Concentration

Concentration means inner vigilance and alertness. There are thieves all around us and within us. Fear, doubt, worry and anxiety are inner thieves that are trying to steal our inner poise and peace of mind. When we learn how to concentrate, it is very difficult for these forces to enter into us. If doubt enters into our mind, the power of concentration will tear doubt to pieces. If fear enters into our mind, the power of concentration will chase away our fear. Right now we are victims to unlit, obscure, destructive thoughts, but a day will come when, on the strength of our concentration, disturbing thoughts will be afraid of us.

Concentration is the mind's dynamic will that operates in us for our acceptance of light and rejection of darkness. It is like a divine warrior in us. What concentration can do in our life of aspiration is unimaginable. It can easily separate Heaven from hell, so that we can live in the constant delight of Heaven and not in the perpetual worries, anxieties and tortures of hell while we are here on earth.

Concentration is the surest way to reach our goal, whether the goal is God-realisation or merely the fulfilment of human desires. A real aspirant sooner or later acquires the power of concentration either through the Grace of God, through constant practice or through his own aspiration.

The soul's indomitable will
When we concentrate we are like a bullet entering into something, or like a magnet pulling the object of con-

centration toward us. At that time we do not allow any thought to enter into our mind, whether it is divine or undivine, earthly or Heavenly, good or bad. In concentration the entire mind has to be focused on a particular object or subject. If we are concentrating on the petal of a flower, we try to feel that nothing else exists in the entire world but the petal. We look neither forward nor backward, upward nor inward; only we try to pierce the object with our one-pointed concentration. This is not an aggressive way of entering into something. This concentration comes directly from the soul's indomitable will, or will power.

When you want to practise concentration on an object, you should choose something that gives you immediate joy. If you have a Master, your Master's picture will give you immediate joy. If you do not have a Master, select something that is very beautiful, divine and pure, like a flower, for example.

> We concentrate with the mind's illumining one-pointedness. We meditate with the heart's expanding vastness. We contemplate with the soul's fulfilling oneness.

Concentrating from the heart
Very often I hear aspirants say that they cannot concentrate for more than five minutes. After five minutes they get a headache or feel that their head is on fire. Why? It is because the power of their concentration is coming from the intellectual mind or, you can say, the disciplined mind. The mind knows that it must not wander; that much knowledge the mind has. But if the mind is to be utilised properly, in an illumined way, then the light of the soul has to come into it. When the light of the soul has entered into the mind, it is extremely easy to concentrate on something for hours. During this time

there will be no thoughts or doubts or fears. No negative forces can enter into the mind if it is surcharged with the soul's light.

When we concentrate we have to feel that our power of concentration is coming from the heart centre and then going up to the third eye. The heart centre is where the soul is located. When we think of the soul at this time, it is better not to form any specific idea of it or try to think of what it looks like. Only we will think of it as God's representative or as boundless light and delight. When we concentrate, we try to feel that the soul's light is coming from the heart and passing through the third eye. Then, with this light, we enter into the object of concentration and identify with it. The final stage of concentration is to discover the hidden, ultimate Truth in the object of concentration.

Glimpsing the Infinite: Meditation

When we concentrate we focus our attention on one particular thing. But when we meditate we feel that we have the capacity deep within us to see many things, deal with many things and welcome many things all at the same time. When we meditate, we try to expand ourselves, like a bird spreading its wings. We try to expand our finite consciousness and enter into the Universal Consciousness where there is no fear, jealousy or doubt but only joy, peace and divine power.

Meditation means our conscious growth into the Infinite. When we meditate what we actually do is enter into a vacant, calm, silent mind and allow ourselves to be nourished and nurtured by Infinity itself. When we are in meditation we want only to commune with God. Now I am speaking in English and you are able to understand me because you know English well. Similarly, when we know how to meditate well, we will be able to commune with God, for meditation is the language we use to speak with God.

A sea of tranquillity

Meditation is like going to the bottom of the sea, where everything is calm and tranquil. On the surface there may be a multitude of waves, but the sea is not affected below. In its deepest depths, the sea is all silence. When we start meditating, first we try to reach our own inner existence, our true existence—that is to say, the bottom of the sea. Then, when the waves come from the outside world, we are not affected. Fear, doubt, worry and all the earthly turmoil will just wash away, because inside us is solid peace. Thoughts cannot trouble us, because our mind is all peace, all silence, all oneness. Like fish in the sea, they jump and swim but leave no mark. So when we are in our highest meditation we feel that we are the sea, and the animals in the sea cannot affect us. We feel that we are the sky, and all the birds flying past cannot affect us. Our mind is the sky and our heart is the infinite sea. This is meditation.

Becoming the Truth: Contemplation

Through concentration we become one-pointed. Through meditation we expand our consciousness into the Vast and enter into its consciousness. But in contemplation we grow into the Vast itself, and its consciousness becomes our very own. In contemplation we are at once in our deepest concentration and our highest meditation. The truth that we have seen and felt in meditation, we grow into and become totally one with in contemplation. When we are concentrating on God, we may feel God right in front of us or beside us. When we are meditating, we are bound to feel Infinity, Eternity and Immortality within us. But when we are contemplating, we will see that we ourselves are God, that we ourselves are Infinity, Eternity and Immortality.

Contemplation means our conscious oneness with the infinite, eternal Absolute. In contemplation the Creator and the creation, the lover and the Beloved, the knower and the known become one. One moment we are the divine lover and God is the Supreme Beloved. The next moment we change roles. In contemplation we become one with the Creator and see the whole universe inside us. At that time when we look at our own existence, we do not see a human being. We see something like a dynamo of light, peace and bliss.

Concentration gives the message of alertness. Meditation gives the message of vastness. Contemplation gives the message of inseparable oneness.

Meditation vs. contemplation

If we meditate on a specific divine quality such as light or peace or bliss, or if we meditate in an abstract way on Infinity, Eternity or Immortality, then all the time we will feel an express train going forward inside us. We are meditating on peace, light or bliss while the express train is constantly moving. Our mind is calm and quiet in the vastness of Infinity, but there is a movement; a train is going endlessly toward the goal. We are envisioning a goal, and meditation is taking us there.

In contemplation it is not like that. In contemplation we feel the entire universe and farthest Goal deep inside ourselves. When we are contemplating we feel that we are holding within ourselves the entire universe with all its infinite light, peace, bliss and truth. There is no thought, no form, no idea.

In contemplation everything is merged into one stream of consciousness. In our highest contemplation we feel that we are nothing but consciousness itself; we are one with the Absolute. But in our highest meditation there is a dynamic movement going on in our consciousness. We are fully aware of what is happening in the inner and the outer world, but we are not affected. In contemplation, too, we are unaffected by what is going on in the inner and outer worlds, but our whole existence has become part and parcel of the universe, which we are holding deep inside us.

How To

Exercises in Concentration

1 **The dot.** If you want to develop the power of concentration, then here is an exercise you can try. First wash your face and eyes properly with cold water. Then make a black dot on the wall at eye level. Stand facing the dot, about ten inches away, and concentrate on it. After a few minutes, try to feel that when you are breathing in, your breath is actually coming from the dot, and that the dot is also breathing in, getting its breath from you. Try to feel that there are two persons: you and the black dot. Your breath is coming from the dot and its breath is coming from you.

In ten minutes, if your concentration is very powerful, you will feel that your soul has left you and entered into the black dot on the wall. At this time try to feel that you and your soul are conversing. Your soul is taking you into the soul's world for realisation, and you are bringing the soul into the physical world for manifestation. In this way you can develop your power of concentration very easily. But this method has to be practised. There are many things which are very easy with practice, but just because we do not practise them we do not get the result.

2 **Vision and reality.** Another exercise you can try is this. First make a very small circle on the wall at eye-level, and inside it make a black dot. It should be black; not blue or red or any other colour. Then stand facing the wall, about three and a half feet away, and focus your attention on the circle. Your eyes should be relaxed and half-open. Let the force of your concentration come from the middle of your forehead. After three or four minutes open your eyes fully and try to feel that, from head to foot, you are all eyes. Your whole physical existence has become nothing but vision, and that vision is focussed on the dot inside the circle. Then start making the object of your concentration smaller. After a few seconds try to feel that your whole body has become as tiny as the dot on the wall. Try to feel that the dot is another part of your own existence. Then enter into the dot, pierce through it and go to the other side. From the other side of the dot, look back and see your own body. Your physical body is on one side, but on the strength of your concentration you have sent your subtle body to the other side of the dot. Through your subtle body you are seeing your physical body, and through your physical body you are seeing your subtle body.

I concentrate for success in my life's journey.
I meditate for progress in my life's journey.
I contemplate for God-process in my life's journey.

When you began to concentrate, your physical body became all vision. At that time the dot was your reality. When you entered into the dot, then vision and reality became one. You were the vision and you were also the reality. When you looked back at yourself from the dot, the process was reversed. At that time you became the vision outside yourself, and the place to which you returned—your body—was the reality. Then, the vision and the reality became one again. When you can see the vision and the reality in this way, your concentration is absolutely perfect. When your power of concentration can bring you to the other side of the point which you were calling reality, at that time your whole existence will be far beyond both vision and reality. And when you can feel that you have transcended your vision and your reality, you will have boundless power.

If you are my disciple, when you concentrate on the black dot inside the circle, you can try to see your own self there—your own face of aspiration. Feel that you exist there and nowhere else. Then try to feel that your existence, your face, your consciousness—everything—have been replaced by mine. Once you feel that your previous existence has been totally replaced by mine, you will have established your inseparable oneness with me, and my will power is bound to come into your life.

3 **My heart-friend.** Just as you can concentrate on the tip of your finger, or on a candle or any other material object, you can also concentrate on your heart. You may close your eyes or look at a wall, but all the time you are thinking of your heart as a dear friend. When this thinking becomes most intense, when it absorbs your entire attention, then you have gone beyond ordinary thinking and entered into concentration. You cannot look physically at your spiritual heart, but you can focus all your attention on it. Then gradually the power of your concentration enters into the heart and takes you completely out of the realm of the mind.

If you do not have purity in abundant measure, if countless earthly desires are in possession of the heart, then before concentrating on the heart you should invoke purity. Purity is the feeling of having a living shrine deep in the inmost recesses of your heart. When you feel the divine presence of an inner shrine, automatically you are purified. At that time your concentration on the heart will be most effective.

4 **The heartbeat of life.** Some seekers like to concentrate on their heartbeat. If you want to do this, do not be afraid that the heart will stop and you will die. If you want to be a real hero in your spiritual life, you can practise concentrating on your heartbeat. This is the golden opportunity for you to enter into the endless life. Each time you hear the sound of your heartbeat, immediately feel there your infinite, immortal life.

5 **The inner flower.** For this exercise you will need a flower. With your eyes half closed and half open, look at the entire flower for a few seconds. While you are concentrating, try to feel that you yourself are this flower. At the same time, try to feel that this flower is growing in the inmost recesses of your heart. Feel that you are the flower and you are growing inside your heart.

Then, gradually try to concentrate on one particular petal of the flower. Feel that this petal which you have selected is the seed-form of your reality-existence. After a few minutes, concentrate on the entire flower again, and feel that it is the Universal Reality. In this way go back and forth, concentrating first on the petal—the seed-form of your reality—and then on the entire flower—the Universal Reality. While you are doing this, please try not to allow any thought to enter into your mind. Try to make your mind absolutely calm, quiet and tranquil.

After some time, please close your eyes and try to see the flower that you have been concentrating on inside your heart. Then, in the same way that you concentrated on the physical flower, kindly concentrate on the flower inside your heart, with your eyes closed.

Exercises in Meditation

1 **The heart-rose.** Kindly imagine a flower inside your heart. Suppose you prefer a rose. Imagine that the rose is not fully blossomed; it is still a bud. After you have meditated for two or three minutes, please try to imagine that petal by petal the flower is blossoming. See and feel the flower blossoming petal by petal inside your heart. Then, after five minutes, try to feel that there is no heart at all; there is only a flower inside you called 'heart'. You do not have a heart, but only a flower. The flower has become your heart or your heart has become a flower.

After seven or eight minutes, please feel that this flower-heart has covered your whole body. Your body is no longer here; from your head to your feet you can feel the fragrance of the rose. If you look at your feet, immediately you experience the fragrance of a rose. If you look at your knee, you experience the fragrance of a rose. If you look at your hand, you experience the fragrance of a rose. Everywhere the beauty, fragrance and purity of the rose have permeated your entire body. When you feel from your head to your feet that you have become only the beauty, fragrance, purity and delight of the rose, then you are ready to place yourself at the Feet of your Beloved Supreme.

2 **A river of consciousness.** When you meditate, try to bring three things into your mind: purity in your entire being, humility in your entire being and gratitude in every limb, in every cell. When you breathe in and breathe out, feel that a river of divine consciousness is flowing through you without any coercion or exertion. Feel that this river of divine consciousness is flowing in and out with constant oneness with the Source, the Supreme.

3 **Offer it to God.** When you breathe in, feel that you are breathing in God's immortal qualities and when you breathe out, feel that you are offering God your ignorance.

Right now we feel that ignorance is our possession. Although we say that ignorance is very bad, we don't want to give it away. But we have to know that ignorance is not our real possession; our real possessions are peace, light and bliss. During your meditation, offer to God your false possessions and receive from God your real possessions. Ask God to take what you have and what you are and to give you what He has and what He is. What you have is aspiration, the inner cry to become divine. What you are is ignorance. Ask God to take both your aspiration and your ignorance and to give you what He has and what He is: Infinity, Eternity and Immortality.

4 **The golden being.** Try to feel that you are inside the Heart of God, the Inner Pilot. Although you have not seen the Supreme, just mentally imagine a human being who is absolutely golden. Imagine that He is right in front of you and you are inside His Heart or in His Lap or at His Feet. Do not think that you are eighteen or forty or sixty years old. Think that you are only one month old and that you are inside the very Heart of the Supreme or in His Lap.

5 **The vastness of the sky.** Keep your eyes half open and imagine the vast sky. In the beginning try to feel that the sky is in front of you; later try to feel that you are as vast as the sky, or that you are the vast sky itself.

After a few minutes please close your eyes and try to see and feel the sky inside your heart. Please feel that you are the universal heart, and that inside you is the sky that you meditated upon and identified yourself with. Your spiritual heart is infinitely vaster than the sky, so you can easily house the sky within yourself.

An Exercise in Contemplation

1 **Hide-and-seek.** Try to imagine a golden being and feel that he is infinitely more beautiful than the most beautiful child that you have ever seen on earth. This being is your Beloved Lord Supreme. You are a divine lover and the golden being is your Beloved Lord Supreme.

Now, try to imagine that your own existence and also that of your Beloved are on the top of a mountain in the Himalayas or at the very bottom of the Pacific Ocean, whichever is easier for you. Once you feel this, then inwardly smile.

After a few seconds please feel that you yourself are the Beloved Supreme and that the golden being is the divine lover. It is like a divine game of hide-and-seek. When you become the Supreme Beloved, the divine lover seeks you, and when you become the divine lover, you search for your Beloved Supreme. One moment you are the supreme lover and the next moment you are the Supreme Beloved.

In the beginning, please do this with your eyes half open. When you become expert, you can close your eyes.

Q&A

Q When I sit down to meditate, I have to concentrate so hard on keeping my mind still that I cannot contact my inner self.

A You may not know it, but you are doing the right thing. When you are trying to make your mind calm and quiet, you are concentrating. In concentration, you try to control your thoughts and emotions. Concentration has to pave the way for meditation. In order to meditate you must have already disciplined your emotional life and restless mind to some extent. When you are successful in chasing away all the thoughts that disturb your mind, sooner or later your inner self will come to the fore, like the blazing sun clearing away the veil of clouds. Right now, the inner sun is overcast with clouds: thoughts, ideas, doubts, fears and so forth. When you can chase them away, you will see that your inner self is shining, bright and radiant, right in front of you.

Q How can one know whether one is doing concentration or meditation?

A When it is concentration, there is tremendous intensity; it is like an arrow entering into a target. If you feel an intense force energising you, then this is the result of your concentration. But in meditation, there is peace and a feeling of vastness all around, especially in the mind. If you feel deep within an immense sea of peace, light and bliss, then that is due to your meditation. Meditation is all peace, poise and vastness. Intensity is there, but the intensity is flooded with luminosity. In concentration there need not be and often is not the highest luminosity.

Also, concentration wants immediate results. It is ready to do anything to achieve its goal. Meditation feels that it has infinite time at its disposal. That does not mean that meditation neglects the fleeting time. No, it appreciates fleeting time, but inside fleeting time it sees endless time. That is why meditation has infinite peace inside it.

Do not give any preference to either experience. If the Supreme wants to concentrate in you and through you, then you will allow it. Again, if He wants to meditate in and through you, that also you will allow.

Q Once we have learned how to meditate, should we no longer practise concentration?

A As a general rule, seekers who are just entering the spiritual life should start with concentration for a few months at least. Once they have learned to concentrate, then meditation becomes easy. But even when you are able to meditate, it is a good idea to concentrate for a few minutes before you start your daily meditation. If you concentrate, you are like a runner who clears the track of obstacles before he starts to run. Once the track is cleared, you can run very fast. At that time you become like an inner express train that stops only at the final destination.

Q After we have finished meditating, how do we go about contemplating?

A Contemplation comes after many years, when one is very advanced in the spiritual life. Contemplation is the highest rung of the inner ladder. Very, very few spiritual aspirants have the capacity to do even limited contemplation, and they certainly cannot do so at their sweet will.

Contemplation must be mastered before God-realisation, so it cannot be ignored or avoided. But, in your case, the necessity for contemplation has not come because your concentration and your meditation are not yet perfect. When your concentration is perfect and your meditation is perfect, at that time your contemplation will also have to be perfected. Then you will really be able to enter into the Highest.

> *How can you succeed in your outer life when you do not have the power of concentration? How can you proceed in your inner life when you do not have the peace of meditation?*

Our prayer gives us a peaceful life. Our meditation gives us a beautiful heart.

Two Wings to Fly: Prayer & Meditation

Chapter 7
Two Wings to Fly: Prayer & Meditation

🍃 I Pray, I Meditate

I pray. Why do I pray? I pray because I need God. I meditate. Why do I meditate? I meditate because God needs me.

When I pray, I think that God is high above me, above my head. When I meditate, I feel that God is deep inside me, inside my heart.

Prayer says, "I am helpless, I am impure, I am weak. I need You, O Lord Supreme, to strengthen me, to purify me, to illumine me, to perfect me, to immortalise me. I need You, O Lord Supreme."

Meditation says, "Lord Supreme, out of Your infinite bounty You have chosen me to be Your instrument to manifest You here on earth in Your own way. You could have chosen somebody else to play the role, but You have granted me the golden opportunity. To You I offer my constant gratitude, my gratitude-heart."

Prayer is purity. It purifies the mind, which is always subject to doubt, fear, worry and anxiety, and is always assailed by wrong thoughts and wrong movements. When we pray, purification takes place in our minds, and purity increases our God-receptivity. In fact, purity is nothing short of God-receptivity. Each time we pray, our inner receptacle becomes large, larger, largest. Then purity, beauty, light and delight can enter into that receptacle and sport together in the inmost recesses of our heart.

Meditation is luminosity. It illumines our heart. When illumination takes place in our heart, insecurity and the sense of want disappear. At that time we sing the song of inseparable oneness with the Universal Consciousness and Transcendental Consciousness. When our heart is illumined, the finite in us enters into the Infinite and becomes the Infinite itself. The bondage of millennia leaves us, and the freedom of infinite Truth and Light welcomes us.

Prayer says to God, "Beloved Supreme, You are mine. I claim You as my own, very own. Do grant me Your divine qualities in boundless measure so that I can be Your perfect instrument here on earth."

Meditation says to God, "O Beloved Supreme, I am Yours. You can utilise me at Your sweet Will at every moment, throughout Eternity. Through me fulfil Yourself here on earth and there in Heaven."

The best definition of prayer is to practise it daily. The best definition of meditation is to experience it soulfully. The best definition of yoga is to live it sincerely. The best definition of God is to love Him, and Him only, unconditionally.

Prayer is something absolutely intense and upward-soaring. When we pray, we feel that our existence is a one-pointed flame soaring upward. From the soles of our feet to the crown of our head, our whole being is invoking and calling upwards. The very nature of prayer is to reach God by going up.

Meditation is something wide and vast that ultimately expands into the Infinite. When we meditate, we throw ourselves into a vast expanse, into an infinite sea of peace and bliss, or we welcome the infinite Vast into us. Prayer rises; meditation spreads. Meditation is constantly growing and expanding into peace, light and delight. When we meditate, we gradually see, feel and grow into the entire universe of light and delight.

Thy Will be done

When we pray, often there is a subtle desire for something, a hankering to get something or to become something. We may call it aspiration because we are praying to become good, or to have something divine which we do not have, or to be free from fear, jealousy, doubt and so forth. But there is always a subtle tendency on our part to push or pull from within.

Also, there is always the feeling of being—let us use the term 'a divine beggar'. We feel that God is high above, while we are down below. We see a yawning gulf between His existence and ours. We are looking up at Him and crying to Him, but we do not know when or to what extent God is going to fulfil our prayers. We feel that we are helpless. We just ask, and then we wait for one drop, two drops or three drops of compassion, light or peace to descend upon us. Sometimes there is a feeling of give-and-take. We say, "Lord, I am giving You my prayer, so now You please do something for me. You please help me, save me, fulfil me."

But in meditation we do not ask God for any help, boon or divine quality; we just enter into the sea of His Reality. At that time God gives us more than we could ever imagine. In prayer we feel that we have nothing and God has everything. In meditation we know that whatever God has, either we also have or we will someday have. We feel that whatever God is, we also are, only we have not yet brought our divinity forward. When we pray, we ask God for what we want. But when we meditate, God showers on us everything that we need. We see and feel that the whole universe is at our disposal. Heaven and earth do not belong to someone else; they are our own reality.

The highest prayer is, "Let Thy Will be done." This is absolutely the highest reach of prayer, and it is also the beginning of meditation. Where prayer stops its journey, meditation begins. In meditation we say nothing, we think nothing, we want nothing. In the meditation-world the Supreme is acting in and through us for His own fulfilment. The prayer-world is always asking for something. But the meditation-world says, "God is not blind or deaf. He knows what He has to do to fulfil Himself in and through me. So I shall just grow into the highest in soulful silence."

Two roads to realisation
Prayer and meditation are like two roads. Prayer is always for our own sake, for our own life, for the near and dear ones in our own small world. If we pray well, God will give us two wings to fly above. But meditation is for the entire world. When we meditate well, we feel our oneness with our own expanded reality. If we can follow the road of meditation, we are hero-warriors. At that time we can carry on our giant shoulders the entire burden of humanity. When we fulfil our meditation-life, we fulfil not only God but also ourselves and the entire world.

For those who want to realise the Highest, I always say that meditation is of paramount importance. But there have been saints in the West who have realised God through prayer only. They did not know the concept of meditation. But the intensity of their prayers and their aspiration carried them into the world of meditation and beyond. Both approaches are effective. When we pray, we go up to God; when we meditate, God comes down to us. Ultimately the result can be the same.

The necessity of prayer
If one becomes advanced in meditation, prayer is not necessary. At that time we will realise that God always knows our needs and cares for us infinitely more than we care for ourselves. Prayer is not necessary, because

we belong to God and are His property. When we renounce our personal claims and surrender ourselves completely, at that time God claims us as His very own and makes us His chosen instruments.

But until we become very advanced in the spiritual life and feel our oneness with God, prayer is necessary. If we get something through prayer, we can tell the world, "I prayed for it; that's why I got it. Look, I have this kind of closeness with my Father!" We are like children who are hungry. We ask our mother for food, and she feeds us. Yes, she would have fed us on her own, but the fact that we ask for food and our mother listens to our request gives us joy. It convinces our minds that she really cares for us. Because of our inner connection and closeness with our mother, we can ask her for whatever we want.

God could do everything for us unconditionally, but this would not give us the same kind of satisfaction. In a race, if you run the whole course, then you will be delighted if you receive a trophy. You ran very fast and finished with so much trouble, and you feel that you have earned the trophy. But if somebody who has just been a spectator gets a trophy, that person will not feel satisfied, because he has done nothing to earn it. God can give everything unconditionally, but we get more satisfaction if He gives us something after we have prayed for it or worked for it.

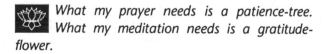 *What my prayer needs is a patience-tree. What my meditation needs is a gratitude-flower.*

We have to know, however, that when we pray we feel that we as individuals are separated from God. We feel that He is at one place and we are somewhere else. At that time we are not in our highest consciousness where we feel that we are one with God. If we feel that we and God are one, then the question of prayer does not arise, for at that time our needs are His needs.

Prayer, we can say, intensifies our intimacy with the Supreme, whereas meditation increases our oneness with the Supreme. First we have to feel that we and God are intimate friends; then we can realise our oneness-reality with God. Before we meditate, if we can pray for a few minutes, we can develop our intimate connection with the Supreme. Then we can meditate to become one with Him.

In the highest spiritual life there is no comparison between meditation and prayer. Meditation is infinitely deeper and wider than prayer. In the West, prayer is used by seekers with considerable efficacy. But a real seeker who wants to go to the Ultimate Beyond must feel that meditation is the higher rung in the ladder to God-realisation. When we meditate, we see, feel and grow into the entire universe of light and delight.

Q&A

Q I would like to know whether I should pray for something I want or whether I should just pray for God's Will to be done.

A To pray for God's Will to be done is the highest form of prayer. But a beginner finds it almost impossible to pray to God sincerely to fulfil him in God's own way. So when the seeker is just starting out, it is advisable for him to pray to God for whatever he feels he needs most, whether it is patience, purity, sincerity, humility, peace and so forth. Then God will give the seeker a little peace, light and bliss, which are the precursors of something infinite that is going to come into his inner being. Once the seeker has received some peace, light and bliss and they have become established to some extent in his inner being, at that time he will have some confidence in God's operation and also in his own life of aspiration.

When one is making very fast progress or is a little advanced, he feels that there is some reality within himself and that this reality is not going to disappoint or desert him. Then he feels that God is fully aware of what he desperately needs and is eager to supply him with those things. When a seeker feels this kind of confidence within him, that is the time for the seeker to pray, "Let Thy Will be done." At that time he can sincerely say, "God, I want to please You only in Your own way."

Prayer is best expressed in my day-to-day life when my prayer has become a spontaneous, self-giving surrender to the Will of God.

Q How can we pray effectively?

A To pray most effectively, your prayer should be outwardly inaudible, but you may form a sentence of a few words that will convince your aspiring mind. The heart is already aspiring, but the mind needs to aspire. So it is better for the prayer to take the form of words.

You may form the sentence by writing it on the tablet of your heart. Then try to see it there. Once the words are written, you can return many times to see them. If you want to repeat the sentence, good, but it is not necessary. When you repeat your prayer you have a choice. Either write it once on the tablet of your heart and read it again and again, or continuously write the same thing—whichever gives you more joy.

Q How can we make our prayer most intense?

A You can make your prayer most intense by using your gratitude-heart. While you are praying, you should feel that the prayer is coming from your heart, and you have to feed the prayer with gratitude. If you do not nourish the prayer with your gratitude-heart, then your prayer will not be intense. Nothing divine will be intense unless and until you are grateful to the Supreme. At every moment your gratitude-heart must feed your inner cry. This will intensify your prayer, your aspiration, your dedication and all your spiritual qualities.

When I pray, I kneel down devotedly and secretly. When I meditate, I lift up my heart soulfully and perfectly.

Q What is the best way to pray for others?

A First, before you even start praying, you should invoke the presence of the Supreme. When you invoke His presence, He will definitely come in a subtle form. You will not see Him in a human body, but you will be able to feel His presence. Inside God's presence, try to see and feel the person for whom you are praying. If you can invoke the Supreme's presence and feel inside His presence those for whom you are praying, that will be the most effective way of helping them through your prayer.

But before asking the Supreme through your prayer to help someone, first ask Him whether you are supposed to pray for that particular person. If you get a message or inner feeling that you should pray for that particular person, only then should you do it. Suppose somebody is very sick and you want to pray to God to cure him.

You have to know that perhaps God wants him to have this experience right now for his own inner development. You have to know that God has infinitely more love for that particular person than you or any other human being could possibly have. If you ask God to cure him, you may only be opposing God's Will. But if you pray for oneness with God's Will, then God may say, "You have become one with My Will. Now I will be happy if you ask me to cure the person."

Q Do you pray sometimes?

A To be quite frank with you, I do not pray; nor do I have any need for meditation, although I do meditate. After one has realised the Highest and become consciously one with the Absolute Supreme, one has no need to pray or meditate. But I have a number of disciples, so I meditate for them as I used to meditate for myself many years ago. When I meditate on them, prayer is automatically there because, in trying to help them in their spiritual awakening, I am invoking God's infinite blessings, light and compassion to offer to them.

 They say that prayer is the daughter of suffering. But I say that prayer is the mother of delight.

I purify my body by chanting God's name. I purify my vital by serving God. I purify my mind by emptying my mind for God. I purify my heart by meditating on God's Compassion-Love.

The Power of Mantra

The Power of Mantra

❦ Chanting: Mantra and Japa

A mantra is an incantation. It can be a syllable, a word, a few words or a sentence. When you repeat a mantra many times, it is called japa. A mantra represents a particular aspect of God, and each mantra has a special significance and inner power.

If you cannot enter into your deepest meditation because your mind is restless, this is an opportunity to utilise a mantra. You can repeat "Supreme" or *Aum* or "God" for a few minutes. Also, if you get an attack on the emotional vital plane and wrong thoughts or wrong vibrations are entering into you, you can repeat *Aum* or the name of the Supreme. In this case try to do it as fast as possible. When you are trying to cleanse your mind of impurities, you must chant as if you were running to catch a moving train. During regular japa, however, just say the mantra in a normal but soulful way. But do not prolong it too much; otherwise, you will not have time to chant the five hundred or six hundred times that may be necessary.

Achieving overall purification
If you want to achieve overall purification of your nature, then japa can be most effective if you do it in a systematic way, step by step. On the first day repeat *Aum* or "Supreme" or whatever mantra your Master has given you five hundred times. The next day repeat it six hundred times; the day after that, seven hundred; and so on, until you reach twelve hundred at the end of one

week. Then begin descending each day until you reach five hundred again. In this way you can climb up the tree and climb down the tree.

Please continue this exercise, week by week, for a month. Whether you want to change your name or not, the world will give you a new name: purity.

While you are doing japa, if you make a mistake and lose track of the number, no harm. Just continue with some likely number. The purpose of counting is to separate your consciousness from other things. When you count, you will not be thinking of someone else or something else. While you are counting, you should try to enter into the world of silence which is deep inside the mantra. Then you will not have to count at all. Your consciousness will be focused on what you are repeating and you will begin to feel that you are meditating only on the inner significance of the mantra.

In most cases it is best to chant a mantra aloud. But after doing this for a few minutes, if you can feel that there is somebody inside—your inner being—who is repeating the mantra on your behalf, then you do not have to chant out loud. In the silence of your heart your inner being will do japa on your behalf.

Japa should be done in the morning or during the day, not just before going to bed. If japa is done when the body is tired and wants to enter into the world of sleep, the mind will just become agitated and lose its one-pointed concentration. You will only be working the mind mechanically, and you will derive no benefit. If japa is not done sincerely and soulfully, it is useless. So it should be done only one hundred, two hundred or at most three hundred times before going to bed. If you meditate before going to bed, you will invoke peace, light and bliss, but if you do japa five hundred to twelve hundred times before going to bed, you will invoke power and energy, and you will not be able to sleep.

Often when you complete your japa, you will hear the mantra being repeated inside your heart. Your mouth is not saying it, but your inner being has started repeating the mantra spontaneously.

The inner sound

During meditation sometimes seekers hear the sound of *Aum*, although they have not said it out loud and nobody in the room has chanted it out loud. This means that inwardly somebody has chanted *Aum* or is chanting it, and the meditation room has preserved the sound.

Chanting a mantra can be done while you are driving or walking along the street or standing in a public place. If you silently chant while walking along the street, you are not withdrawing; only you are trying to protect yourself from the unaspiring world. You are increasing your inner strength and inner capacity. Then, when you are inwardly strong, you will no longer have to chant; you can just move around and not be disturbed.

Any method of spiritual discipline will have two inevitable and inseparable wings: absolute patience and firm resolution.

If you are trying to maintain a high consciousness when you are in a public place, it may be difficult for you to go deep within and bring peace to the fore. But even when you are surrounded by the noise and bustle of the outer world, you can easily bring forward a louder sound. This louder sound is not a destructive sound but one that contains indomitable power. It gives you a feeling of how potentially great and divine you are. If you can bring to the fore the divine inner sound, which comes from your heart, or if you can enter into that inner sound, then you will see that the outer noise of the world is no match for it. To your surprise, you will see that the sounds which disturbed you one minute ago will not bother you anymore. On the contrary, you will get a sense of achievement because instead of hearing noise you will hear divine music that is produced by your inner being.

The Essence of *Aum*

Aum is a single, indivisible sound; it is the vibration of the Supreme. *Aum* is the seed-sound of the universe, for with this sound God set into motion the first vibration of His creation. The most powerful of all mantras is *Aum; Aum* is the mother of all mantras. At every second God is creating Himself anew inside *Aum*. Without birth is *Aum,* without death is *Aum*. Nothing else but *Aum* existed, exists and will forever exist.

Aum is a single Sanskrit character represented in English by three letters, but pronounced as one syllable. The syllable *Aum* is indivisible, but each portion of it represents a different aspect of the Supreme. The 'A' represents and embodies the consciousness of God the Creator, the 'U' embodies the consciousness of God the Preserver and the 'M' embodies the consciousness of God the Transformer. Taken together, *Aum* is the spontaneous cosmic rhythm with which God embraces the universe.

The sound of *Aum* is unique. Generally we hear a sound when two things are struck together. But *Aum* needs no such action. It is *anahata,* or unstruck; it is the soundless sound. A Yogi or spiritual Master can hear *Aum* self-generated in the inmost recesses of his heart.

There are many ways to chant *Aum*. When you chant it loudly, you feel the omnipotence of the Supreme. When you chant it softly, you feel the delight of the Supreme. When you chant it silently, you feel the peace of the Supreme.

The universal *Aum* put forth by the Supreme is an infinite ocean. The individual *Aum* chanted by man is a drop in that ocean, but it cannot be separated from the ocean, and it can claim the infinite ocean as its very own. When man chants *Aum,* he touches and calls forth the cosmic vibration of the supreme Sound.

It is best to chant *Aum* out loud, so its sound can vibrate even in your physical ears and permeate your entire body. This will convince your outer mind and give you a greater sense of joy and achievement. When chanting out loud, the 'M' sound should last at least three times as long as the 'AU' sound.

No matter how grave a person's mistakes, if he chants *Aum* many times from the inmost depths of his heart, the omnipotent Compassion of the Supreme will forgive him. In the twinkling of an eye the power of *Aum* transforms darkness into light, ignorance into knowledge and death into Immortality.

Aum has infinite power; just by repeating *Aum* one can realise God. Everything that God has and everything that God is, within and without, *Aum* can offer, because *Aum* is at once the life, the body and the breath of God.

Q You said we can increase our purity by repeating *Aum* five hundred times a day. But for me to repeat *Aum* five hundred times a day is very difficult. Can you advise me what to do?

A If it is difficult for you to do it at one stretch, then you can do it in segments. At ten different times you can repeat it only fifty times. Say that during the day you want to drink ten glasses of water. If you try to drink all ten glasses of water at once, you will not be able to do it. So you drink one glass now and after an interval of an hour or two another glass. Then easily you can drink ten glasses of water. Instead of chanting *Aum* five hundred times all at once, early in the morning you can repeat it fifty times. Then, in an hour's time, do another fifty. Each hour if you repeat *Aum* fifty times, it won't take you more than a minute or two each time. Since you can easily offer two minutes in an hour to God, you can do your chanting in this way.

Music has and also is the key to unlock the Heart-Door of the Supreme.

Music & Meditation: Sound & Silence

Music & Meditation: Sound & Silence

❦ A Universal Language

Music is the inner or universal language of God. I do not speak French or German or Italian, but if music is played from any of those countries, immediately the heart of the music enters into my heart, or my heart enters into the music. At that time no outer communication is needed; the inner communion of the heart is enough. My heart is communing with the heart of the music, and in our communion we become inseparably one.

Meditation and music cannot be separated. When we cry from the inmost recesses of our heart for peace, light and bliss, that is the best type of meditation. Next to meditation is music, soulful music, the music that stirs and elevates our aspiring consciousness. We cannot meditate twenty-four hours a day, but we can meditate, perhaps, for two hours a day. At other times we can play music or listen to music. When we play or hear soulful music, psychic music, immediately we are transported to a higher realm of consciousness. When we play music soulfully, we go high, higher, highest.

Each time we hear soulful music, we get inspiration and delight. In the twinkling of an eye, music can elevate our consciousness. But if we also pray and meditate, then we are undoubtedly more illumined and fulfilled than a music-lover who is not consciously leading a spiritual life. Each spiritual musician is consciously spreading God's light on earth. God is the cosmic Player, the eternal Player, and we are His instruments. But there comes a time in the process of our evolution when we feel that we have become totally one with Him. At that time, we are no longer instruments; we ourselves are musicians, divine musicians. It is the Supreme who makes the proper instrument. Then, it is He who inspires the player to play properly.

Let us not try to understand music with our mind. Let us not even try to feel it with our heart. Let us simply and spontaneously allow the music-bird to fly in our heart-sky. While flying, it will unconditionally reveal to us what it has and what it is. What it has, is Immortality's message. What it is, is Eternity's passage.

Q&A

Q Can some kinds of music cause us to feel upset and change our spiritual condition?

A Yes. There is some music that is really destructive to our inner being. This music comes from the gross physical or the lower vital. Undivine music tries to awaken our lower vital consciousness and throw us into a world of excitement. The spiritual person will immediately be affected by this music.

Music has tremendous power. With fire we can burn ourselves, or we can cook and do many other good things. It is the same with music. Divine music immediately elevates our consciousness, whereas undivine music immediately lowers our consciousness and tries to destroy our sincere inner cry for a better, spiritual life. Vital music brings our consciousness down. For a few fleeting moments or hours we get a kind of pleasure; but then this pleasure takes us into a lower vital consciousness where temptation looms large. From the temptation-world we enter into the frustration-world, and from the frustration-world we enter into the destruction-world.

We all know that vital music is most appreciated all over the world. Psychic music is not very widely appreciated, and very few people appreciate the soul's music. They feel that it is like a stranger entering into their consciousness. But this is actually because spiritual music awakens the eternal tenant, the soul, that is deep within them waiting to come to the fore.

Q Can we use music to help us in our spiritual life?

A We can definitely use music to help us in our spiritual life. Music and the spiritual life are like twin brothers; we cannot separate them. How can we separate two fingers, two eyes? They live side by side. If one eye is not functioning well, then we feel that our vision is imperfect. Music and the spiritual life can easily go together; one complements the other. Music helps the spiritual seeker to go deep within to get the utmost satisfaction from life, from truth, from reality. The spiritual life, in turn, helps music to offer its capacity and its strength, which is the soul's light, to the world at large.

Q What does 'soulful' mean in relation to music?

A What do we mean by soulful music? If you say it is the music that embodies the soul, then I wish to say that you are mistaken. You have to feel that soulful music is the light that wants to express itself in a divine way. Even as darkness wants to manifest its authority on earth, light also wants to manifest its reality and divinity in a specific way. Light is the soul of everything. Light is the soul of music, the soul of love, and the soul of all art. When light divinely manifests itself in the form of music, it is the music of the soul.

Soulful music is the music that immediately elevates our consciousness to the highest. Soulful music takes us into the world of aspiration. From aspiration we enter into the world of realisation, where our inner existence is flooded with light and delight.

Soulful music is the music that wants to eventually transform our consciousness. It carries us into the Universal Consciousness and makes us feel that we are in tune with the highest, with the deepest, with the farthest.

It also makes us feel that God Himself is the Supreme Musician. When we play soulful music, we come to realise that we are not the musician; we are just an instrument. We are like a piano, violin or guitar, and it is God who is constantly playing on us. If we really play soulful music, we will feel that we are the instrument, and somebody else is singing and playing in and through us. That somebody is our Inner Pilot, the Supreme.

 God the Creator is the Supreme Musician and God the creation is the supreme music.

When we listen to soulful music, or when we ourselves play soulful music, immediately our inner existence climbs up high, higher, highest. It climbs up and enters into the Beyond, which is constantly trying to help us, guide us, mould us and shape us into our true transcendental image, our true divinity. When we hear soulful music or play a soulful piece of music, we feel a kind of inner thrill in our entire existence. From the soles of our feet to the crown of our head we feel that a river is flowing through us, a river of illumined consciousness.

Next to deep prayer or meditation, music is of paramount importance in our spiritual life. Meditation is like a direct route, or shortcut, to the goal. Music is a road that is absolutely clear: it may be a little longer, but it is quite clear of obstacles. If one can play soulful music or hear soulful music, the power of his own meditation increases. Music, soulful music, adds to our aspiration. Similarly, if a spiritual seeker wants to be a musician, even if he does not have a musical background, he will be able to be a good musician because prayer and meditation contain all capacities. You may never have studied music, but if you pray and meditate soulfully, then inside your prayer, inside your meditation, by the Grace of the Supreme, the power of music will loom large.

Q How do we know if music is spiritual and if the musician is aspiring?

A Whether or not the musician is aspiring is not your business. That is only God's business. Somebody may appear to be spiritual, but if his music brings your consciousness down, then he is not playing spiritual music. When you hear music, if it lifts your consciousness, then you will know that it is spiritual music. Sometimes the musician is aspiring and also he is playing spiritual music; at that time you are very fortunate, because you get inspiration from both the music and the musician.

Q What is the best way to become one with soulful music?

A The best way to become one with soulful music is to have the firm inner conviction while listening to it that as you are breathing in, the breath is immediately entering directly into your soul. And with the breath, you have to feel that the Universal Consciousness, divine Reality, divine Truth is also entering. Then, when you breathe out, try to feel that you are breathing out the ignorance that is covering your soul. Feel that the veils of ignorance are being lifted and discarded. If you can consciously imagine and feel this, it is the best way to become one with soulful music.

Music is God's dream. We don't have to know what it looks like or what it does. Its very existence keeps us alive.

The more you can offer gratitude to the Supreme Pilot within you, the more and the sooner you will increase your receptivity.

Receptivity: Opening to the Light

Chapter 10
Receptivity:
Opening to the Light

❦ What Is Receptivity?

Receptivity is the flow of cosmic energy and cosmic light. Receptivity is the capacity to absorb and hold the divine gifts that the Supreme showers upon you during your meditation. If you want to be receptive, when you sit down to meditate, consciously try to bring light into your being. Once you have brought light inside, direct it to the right place, the spiritual heart. Then try to grow into that light.

If you feel that you have a little receptivity, then cry for more. Do not be satisfied with the receptivity that you have. Today if it is a tiny pool, then make it into a pond, then into a lake, and finally into a vast ocean. Receptivity can be expanded gradually and endlessly. But without receptivity you will not be able to achieve anything in your spiritual life, even from countless hours of meditation.

One way to increase your receptivity is to be like a child. If the mother says to the child, "This is good," the child has no tendency to think it is bad. No matter how advanced you are in the spiritual life, you can make the fastest progress by having a childlike attitude, a sincere and genuine childlike feeling.

Gratitude
The easiest and most effective way to increase your receptivity is to offer your deepest gratitude to the

Supreme each day before you meditate. Many of your near and dear ones are not following the spiritual life, but you have accepted the spiritual life. How is it possible? It is possible because the Supreme inside you has given you the aspiration, whereas there are many, many people who are still not aspiring. You should feel that He has selected you to be spiritual. Because He has given you aspiration, you have every reason to offer Him your gratitude. He will be able to give you more receptivity if He sees that every day you are increasing your gratitude-capacity.

When you offer gratitude to God, immediately your inner vessel becomes large. Then God is able to pour more of His blessings into you or enter more fully into you with His own divine Existence. God is infinite, but only according to our receptivity can He enter into us. God is like sunlight. If I leave the curtains open, sunlight will come in. If I keep all the curtains closed, it cannot come in. The more curtains we open, the more God enters into us with infinite light. When we offer gratitude, immediately God's light comes pouring into our being.

Gratitude means self-offering to one's highest self. Your gratitude is not going to somebody else; it is going to your own highest self. Gratitude helps you identify and feel your oneness with your own highest reality.

You should always be grateful to the Inner Pilot, the Supreme. When you are grateful, your receptivity automatically increases.

 Every morning try to greet God with only one thing: an ever-increasing gratitude-gift.

How To

1 **A receptive place.** One way to get immediate receptivity is to repeat the word "Supreme" in silence over and over again, as fast as possible. First select one place in your body—let us say your third eye—and concentrate there while repeating "Supreme" as fast as possible. Then select another spot and do the same thing. It is better to go from the top downward than from the bottom upward. The place you concentrate on does not have to be a psychic centre. It can be any place you want. If you can do this in seven different places in your body, at one particular place you are bound to find yourself receptive.

2 **A child's cry.** To create receptivity when you do not have it, try to make yourself feel that you are only three years old—a mere baby. You have no mother, no father, nobody at all to protect you, and you are alone in a forest on a very dark night. All around you is darkness. Death is dancing right in front of you, and nobody is there to help you. Then what will you do? You will cry to God from the very depths of your heart, with absolute sincerity. When that kind of inner cry comes, the Supreme is bound to open your heart and make you receptive.

3 **Depend on God.** You can increase your receptivity if you feel that you are extremely helpless without the Supreme, and that with the Supreme, you are everything. This idea, this truth you can write on the tablet of your heart. Try to feel that your inner existence and your outer existence entirely depend on the Su preme. If you feel that your entire existence is meaningless and useless if He is not within you to guide you, to mould you, to shape you, and at the same time to fulfil Himself in you and through you, then your receptivity will expand. Try to feel that you are the chosen child of the Supreme just because He is utilising you, but if you are utilising yourself with your own ego and pride, then you are thousands of miles away from Him. The moment you are away from Him, you are nothing; but the moment you are one with Him with your dedication, devotion and surrender, you are everything. When you feel that you are one with Him, automatically your receptivity expands.

4 **Inner joy.** Another way to expand your receptivity during your meditation is to try to consciously feel inner joy. If you cannot feel inner joy immediately, then try to imagine for a few seconds or a few minutes that you have it. This will not be false. Your imagination will intensify your aspiration and help you to bring forward true inner joy in the course of time. The very nature of inner joy is expansion. When you expand, your receptivity will automatically increase, like a vessel that keeps getting larger.

Q I'm not as receptive in meditation as I would like to be. Why is this?

A Sometimes this happens because our consecration to the Supreme is not yet complete. Sometimes the mind resists, sometimes the vital resists and sometimes the physical or even the subtle physical resists. If there is any such resistance, negative forces can enter us, and our receptivity is lessened. Until we are really sure whether we want the life of desire or the life of aspiration, negative forces will stand between our desire and our aspiration. These forces are always on the alert. They try to separate our aspiration from our desire. Then they try to strengthen our desire and kill our aspiration, and very often they succeed. But a spiritually alert person will take aspiration and enter into desire in order to transform it. If desire enters into aspiration, then aspiration is ruined. If aspiration enters into desire, at that time desire is transformed.

At other times you may not be receptive because you have become too secure; you have become complacent. You do not feel an inner cry because you are satisfied with your material possessions or with the things that you already have in your inner life. Once you are satisfied with what you have, why should you cry for something more? When you have this kind of complacent feeling, your inner cry ceases, and your receptivity also comes to an end.

If you say no to your wrong thoughts and yes to your inspiration to become God's perfect instrument, then boundless receptivity will immediately be yours.

Chapter 11

Aspiration-efforts always supply satisfaction-results. It may take time, at times, but the results are unmistakably sure.

Am I Meditating Well?

❦ What Is a Good Meditation?

Seekers often ask how they can tell whether they are meditating properly or whether they are just deceiving themselves or having mental hallucinations. It is very easy to know. If you are meditating properly, you will get spontaneous inner joy. Nobody has given you good news, nobody has brought you any gifts, nobody has appreciated or admired you, nobody has done anything for you, but you will have an inner feeling of delight. If this happens, then you know that you are meditating properly. But if you feel a mental tension or disturbance, then you will know that the kind of meditation that you are doing is not meant for you.

If you are enjoying mental hallucination, you will feel that peace is within and restlessness is without. You are yearning for peace, light and bliss, but outwardly you are feeling a volcanic turbulence. If you are having a real meditation, a sublime meditation, then you are bound to feel peace within and without. If it is soulful meditation, you will feel your eternal existence; you will feel that you are of Eternity and for Eternity. This feeling you cannot get from a mental hallucination.

There is also another way that you can know. If you are actually entering into a higher plane, you will feel that your body is becoming very light. Although you don't have wings, you will almost feel that you can fly. In fact, when you have reached a very high world, you will actually see a bird inside you that can easily fly just as real birds do.

When it is your imagination, you will get a very sweet feeling for a few minutes; then immediately dark or frustrating thoughts will come into you. You will say, "I studied so hard, but I did not do well in my examination," or "I worked so hard in the office today, but I could not please my boss." These negative forces in the form of frustration will immediately come in. Or doubt will enter, and you may say, "How can I meditate so well when yesterday I did so many wrong things? How can God be pleased with me? How can I be having a high meditation?" But if it is really a high meditation, you will feel that your whole existence, like a divine bird, is soaring high, higher, highest. While you are having this feeling there will be no sad thoughts, no frustrating thoughts and no doubts. You will be flying in the sky of delight where all is joy, peace and bliss.

You can also know whether you had a good meditation by the way you feel afterwards. If peace, light, love and joy have come to the fore from within as a result of your meditation, then you will know that you have meditated well. If you have a good feeling for the world, if you see the world in a loving way in spite of its teeming imperfections, then you will know that your meditation was good. And if you have a dynamic feeling right after meditation, if you feel that you have come into the world to do something and become something—to grow into God's very image and become His dedicated instrument—this indicates that you have had a good meditation. But the easiest way to know if you have had a good meditation is to feel whether peace, light, love and delight have come to the fore from within.

You are now more than ready because your aspiration-bird is flying high above your mind's binding and blinding confusion-clouds.

Am I Meditating Well?

Don't be discouraged

Please do not be disturbed if you cannot meditate well in the beginning. Even in the ordinary life, God alone knows how many years one must practise in order to become very good at something. If an accomplished pianist thinks of what his standard was when he first began to play, he will laugh. It is through gradual progress that he has achieved his present musical height. In the spiritual life also, you may find it difficult to meditate in the beginning. But do not try to force yourself. Ten minutes early in the morning is enough. Gradually your capacity will increase. If you practise every day, you will make progress in your inner life.

Still, every day you cannot eat the most delicious meal. Today you may eat delicious food, and then for three or four days you may eat very simple food. But as long as you are eating, you know that you are sustaining your body. Similarly, if you have a good meditation one day, and the following day you find that you are not able to meditate well, do not become frustrated, and do not try to force yourself to meditate. When your meditation time is over, do not feel miserable even for a moment because you could not meditate. If you are displeased with yourself, then you are making a great mistake. If you cannot meditate on a particular day, try to leave the responsibility with God. If one day you cannot meditate well, feel that some other day the Supreme will again give you the blessing, inspiration and aspiration to meditate extremely well. But if you are disturbed or irritated, some of the progress that you made yesterday or the day before will be diminished or nullified. The best thing is to be calm, quiet and steady in your spiritual life. Then definitely you will continue to make progress in your meditation and in your inner life.

Q&A

Q I often find that the quality of my meditation goes up and down. I always hope that I will not fall down again, but it happens constantly.

A In the beginning everybody experiences ups and downs in the spiritual life. When a child is learning to walk, in the beginning he stumbles and falls again and again. But after a while he learns to walk properly, and finally to run. Eventually he can run as fast as his capacity will allow. But a small child cannot expect to run as fast as his father does, because his father has much more capacity.

You experience ups and downs in your meditation. When you are up, you have to feel that you are getting a glimpse of your eventual capacity. When you are down, you should simply feel that this is only a temporary incapacity. Just because you see that those who are more advanced than you in the spiritual life are running, you must not be discouraged. Once upon a time they also stumbled.

Right now the sky may be full of clouds, but a day will come when the sun will shine again with its full effulgence. When you experience low moments of fear, of doubt, of lack of aspiration, you should feel that these won't last forever. Like a child who has fallen, you must try to stand up again. Someday you will be able to walk, then run, and finally run the fastest without falling.

Q. When you meditate and you cry for something, should you also make an effort to achieve it, or just let it take place naturally?

A At the beginning you have to make a personal effort; later it becomes spontaneous. Unless and until it becomes spontaneous, you have to make the personal effort. When a sprinter starts a race, his hands make such a vigorous movement. In the beginning he consciously moves his arms and hands very fast. He is making strong personal effort. But after fifty or sixty metres, when he is going at top speed, everything becomes spontaneous. At that time he is not striving to move his arms. But at the start, he did.

It is like sailing a boat. Before you start you move this thing and adjust that thing. You have to do all kinds of things at the beginning. While you are getting ready, you are very dynamic. But that is only your preparation. Still the boat is near the shore. It is only when you are actually well on your way that the boat can sail without your constant personal effort. In your meditation this spontaneous movement is an act of Grace from above.

If you are sincere, then you will say that at the very beginning of your journey God's Grace also descended. Otherwise, you would not have been inspired even to enter into the boat. But when you start out, you feel that you are making a tremendous personal effort. But there comes a time when you realise that this personal effort is nothing other than Compassion from above. Why are you getting up early to pray and meditate, whereas your friends are still wallowing in the pleasures of lethargy? It is because God's Grace has descended into you. So the deeper you go, the clearer it becomes that God's Grace enables you to make progress through your personal effort. Either God is pleased with you, or out of His infinite Compassion He is helping you.

Personal effort is of paramount importance at the beginning, because at that time we don't feel that God is our unconditional friend. As human beings, we always say that if I give you something, then you will give me something in return. But if I don't give you anything, then you are under no obligation to give me anything. But God is not like that. God gives unconditionally, whether we claim Him as our own or not. This moment I may pray to God to fulfil my desire. But the next moment, after He fulfils my desire, immediately I will say, "Oh, I don't need You. I don't want to be Your child." But God cannot do that. God always claims us as His own no matter how bad we are, because He sees that in hundreds or thousands or millions of years, He will make us perfect. A child, at his sweet will, can leave his parents; but can the parents leave the child? Impossible! Similarly, I can disown God, my eternal Father, because I am angry with Him or because He has not fulfilled my desires. But He will never disown me, because I am His child.

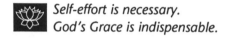 *Self-effort is necessary.*
God's Grace is indispensable.

So personal effort is necessary because we do not feel that God is constantly loving us and blessing us unconditionally. Once we can feel that He is doing everything for us unconditionally, then personal effort is not necessary. Just because we don't have that kind of feeling, so-called personal effort is of paramount importance. But when we become sincere, when we become humble, and especially when we become pure, at that time we will feel that it is God who has inspired us to exercise our personal effort. So credit goes to God from the beginning to the end. In the beginning we give 50 percent of the credit to ourselves, because we got up to pray and meditate, and 50 percent to God, because He responded to our prayers and inspired us during our meditation. But if we are sincere, devoted and abso-

Am I Meditating Well?

lutely pure, then we will say that 100 percent of the credit goes to God.

Q Sometimes during my morning meditation, I fall into a doze—not a sound sleep, but just a doze. Is this a bad thing?

A Unfortunately, it is not a good thing. It is not sound sleep, but you are not fully awake either. When you meditate, you have to be absolutely dynamic. Do not allow sleepiness to enter into you. When you sit down to meditate, feel that you are entering into the battlefield where you have to fight against ignorance, imperfection and death.

Unfortunately, many seekers do not get enough inspiration to energise them for morning meditation. Some mornings you get inspiration all at once; other days you do not get any inspiration at all. If the fire is already burning inside, you do not have to do anything. But when there is no fire, what do you do? The best thing is to breathe in deeply a few times before you meditate and make your whole body energetic. This dynamic energy will help you enter into meditation. If possible, take a small quantity of hot juice or hot milk before you begin your meditation also.

Q How can I keep myself from falling asleep after about five minutes of meditation?

A First of all, before you start meditating please breathe in deeply a few times. With each breath, try to feel that a stream of energy is entering into you. Then try to feel that you are breathing in through different parts of your body: your eyes, your ears, your forehead, your shoulders, the crown of your head and so on. Feel that each of these places is a door, and when you breathe in feel that you are opening this door. At that time, energy enters into you from the Universal Consciousness.

Then try to invoke the power aspect of the Supreme. Do not invoke peace or light; only try to bring forward divine power from within or bring it down from above. This divine power will make you feel that your body is burning with fever, although you are not actually running a temperature, and immediately you will feel energised. You can also imagine a blue-green forest or field, and feel that you are walking through it. Then, no matter how tired you are, you will feel energised.

You can also pinch yourself as hard as possible, and try to feel that somebody else is pinching you. While you are pinching yourself, you have to know that it is your conscious self that is pinching your unconscious self. But you have to feel that another person is doing the pinching.

Another technique is to repeat the name of the Supreme as fast as possible. With tremendous concentration see how many times you can repeat "Supreme" with each breath. The power inside the repetition of this name will inundate your whole being and you are bound to feel a new flow of life-energy.

At meditation time always try to feel inside you a dynamic and progressive movement, but not an aggressive one. If there is a dynamic and progressive movement, then you cannot fall asleep. Inside you, feel that a train is speeding towards the destination. Feel that you yourself are an express train with only one destination. The driver of that train is constantly repeating God's name to derive energy, strength, stamina and all divine qualities. An express train stops only at the final goal, the end of its journey; on the way it does not stop at all. Your goal will be to reach or achieve a profound meditation.

Q Sometimes it seems like I spend my whole time trying to keep myself awake and I don't really meditate.

A Lethargy and sleep come during meditation because sincere interest is lacking. If sincere interest is there, there will be no tendency to sleep. When a student wants to be first in school, when he has a real, sincere interest, then he studies without being forced by his parents. But some students feel that if they just pass the examination, that is more than enough. If this is their feeling, then they do not have any energetic drive or enthusiasm for their school work.

You should always try to be eager and enthusiastic about meditation. If you feel that you cannot meditate for half an hour, then plan to meditate for ten minutes. Then you will feel, "Oh, only ten minutes. Easily I can do that." If your goal is very near, then you will give it all your energy. If it is quite far, you will say, "Oh God! To keep running at top speed for such a long time is impossible." But anybody can meditate for ten minutes. If you have to run twenty miles, you will be scared to death. But if you see that the goal is within sight, then you will say, "Oh, I can easily reach it. Let me run as fast as possible."

Q If we feel tired when we sit down to meditate, how can we energise ourselves so that we don't fall asleep?

A When you feel that you are tired, exhausted, please take several deep breaths quietly and try to feel that you are breathing in from various places in your body. Try to feel that you are breathing in through the eyes, the ears, the forehead, through the crown of the head, through the shoulders and so on. When you are breathing in, if you are conscious of your breath, then you will not feel sleepy. But being conscious of your breath does not mean that you will make a sound. You will just feel that a stream of energy is entering into you with every breath.

Feel that every place you are breathing in is a door. Each time you breathe in, you open a door here, there or somewhere else. Naturally, when you open the door, light also enters, and light is another form of energy.

When you are meditating very well, you may feel that you are spontaneously doing this—drawing energy not only through your nose, but through your head and other places. Energy is available everywhere, and that universal energy wants to enter into you by various doors. Naturally, the more energy you can draw inside you, the higher will be your meditation.

How to conquer fear? With oneness within and oneness without. In oneness-light there can be no fear.

Q When I try to meditate, there is something that holds me back.

A The thing that holds you back is fear. If you want the wealth which is deep inside you, then you have to dive within bravely. Only if you have inner courage can you receive the inner wealth. Fear of the unknown and the unknowable prevents you from diving deep within. But what is unknowable today becomes merely unknown tomorrow, and the day after tomorrow it becomes known.

The vastness of truth will never harm you. It will only embrace and fulfil you. You feel afraid of something because you do not feel that that particular thing is part of you. But through meditation you establish your con-

Am I Meditating Well?

scious oneness with the infinite Vast. At that time you see and feel that everything is part of you. So why should you be afraid?

Q I feel a pressure in my forehead when I meditate. What causes this and how can I stop it?

A The reason you feel pressure in your forehead is because you are meditating in the wrong place; you are meditating in the mind rather than the heart. You want to play a game, but unfortunately you have gone to the wrong playing field. When you feel pressure in your head or your forehead during meditation, it means that your mind has pulled down light and power beyond its capacity. The door to your consciousness is closed, so you are trying to break through the ceiling and pull God into your room. At that time, poor God is entering into an unprepared, unreceptive and unillumined vessel. Naturally the vessel resists, and then you get a headache.

You may also feel pressure because your mind-vessel is filled with impure thoughts and ideas. By sheer will you are trying to kill these undivine thoughts, and again the resistance of the mind causes you pain. The pressure can also mean that there is an obstruction such as fear inside you. When the mind-vessel is filled with impure thoughts and you pull down peace, light and bliss, you unconsciously become frightened. You never expected these things to be so brilliant and divine. Your mind is filled with all kinds of obscure thoughts and impurities, and suddenly divine peace, light and bliss come. At that time they seem like strangers to you, so you resist them. You are driving at top speed and suddenly you feel fear, so you try to stop.

When you feel this kind of pressure, what you should do is immediately focus your attention on your heart. Feel that you do not have a head at all; you have only the heart's soft, sweet feeling of oneness with God, your Inner Pilot. In the heart there is no fear or resistance. No matter how intensely you meditate in the heart, no matter how much peace, light and bliss you draw into the heart, you will never feel tension or pressure. There will only be joy, love and a feeling of oneness.

The safest and best way to meditate is in the heart. But if you want to use the mind, then you have to try to make the mind very calm, quiet, pure and receptive. Always feel that inside the aspiring mind there is a vessel that you can enlarge with your sincere aspiration. Try to make the vessel very large so that it can hold more purity and luminosity. But do not try to pull anything. Only let the divine Grace flow in and through you by praying and meditating most soulfully. Then you will not feel pressure or tension in your head.

Q I don't think that I am pulling, but still I get a headache when I meditate in the morning.

A In your particular case, you are meditating on the wrong thing. You are meditating on divine power, but because your inner vessel is not pure enough, instead of power, an aggressive quality comes into you. This aggression you feel as a headache. So when you meditate in the morning, you should meditate on peace. Inundate your inner and outer being with peace; then you will not get a headache. Peace itself is power; it can solve all your problems.

Q Sometimes, even though I concentrate on my heart, my head pulls down energy and I can't seem to stop it, and I just end up with a headache. Is there any way I can get back to the heart?

A The pain that you are feeling in your head is the result of resistance. What is happening is that your heart is receiving through the mind. Something is coming from above and is trying to enter into the heart, but the mind is not allowing the heart to receive fully. The mind allows the heart to receive to some extent; that is why the force is coming through the mind. But then the mind becomes jealous of the heart and it starts resisting.

At that time try to feel that inside the heart there is something which is infinitely more powerful than the mind. It is the soul, which has immense power. So bring forward your soul's inner strength and say to the mind, "You allowed me to remain quiet for a few minutes, and I am grateful. But I am still praying and meditating, I am still crying for peace, light and bliss, and now you are not allowing me to continue." Then just grab the mind and pull it into the flood of the heart.

The mind is like a naughty child. Previously it was asleep, so the mother was able to remain silent and pray to God. But now the child is awake and it wants to cause mischief. It does not want to allow the mother to aspire any longer. So what will the mother do? She will threaten the child and say, "I am still praying, I am still meditating. You must not disturb me, or I will punish you."

As long as the mind allows you to meditate, you do not have to worry. But when it starts bothering you and creating pain, that means that it does not want to allow you to receive more peace, light and bliss from above. So you have to use your soul's power and pull it into the heart.

Q When I was meditating I felt really tense. My head was hurting and I felt I was pulling. What should I do in a case like that?

If you get that kind of tense feeling, immediately breathe in and out very quickly. When the rhythm of your breathing increases, the tension goes away. Try to feel that you are climbing up a flight of stairs or a ladder that has many rungs. As you climb up you are breathing in. If you feel this ascent, then tension goes away. Tension comes when you are stuck at one place. But when you are climbing, you are like a bird flying up into the sky. When the bird is soaring, where is the tension? Similarly, if you are climbing up, there will be no tension.

Q I find your meditations very hard for me. I come in feeling beautiful. Then I feel all this pain coming into my heart and into my head. Why does this happen?

A It is not any negative force that is entering into you. Your difficulty is that when you come to our meditations, you try to pull far beyond your capacity. When I am on stage, the whole stage is flooded with light. When you sit and look at me, you try to pull this light. It is as if you are in a shop and you see all sorts of most beautiful things. Like a greedy fellow you want to buy everything, but you have in your pocket only five cents. When you try to pull beyond the capacity of your receptivity, at that time you get pain in your head or your heart.

Q Very often when I am concentrating on my heart centre during meditation, I find that my breathing is very heavy and distracting.

A In your case, you are straining your eyes while you are meditating. Your eyes are tight and stiff, and the pressure falls on your heart centre. This is very harmful to your aspiration. If you can keep your eyes normal and relaxed while you are meditating, this pressure will go away. You can keep your eyes open or closed; only don't make them unnaturally stiff.

I shall tolerate the world, I shall. Only by tolerating the world shall I be able to help my mind to ascend and my heart to transcend.

Q When I get upset with someone who does something to me, I can't meditate the way I want to. How can I overcome this?

A When you are upset, naturally you cannot meditate. You cannot welcome a friend and an enemy into your house at the same time. Your enemy is your agitation and anger, and your friend is meditation.

Suppose someone does something to you and you become angry with him. Even when several hours have elapsed and you have forgotten your anger, it can still pull you down. You have forgotten, but you have not forgiven. Unless you have forgiven, you have not illumined your anger. Sometimes you will quarrel with the members of your family and then go to sleep. The next morning you will find that you cannot meditate. You have totally forgotten the incident, but while you were sleeping the strength and velocity of your anger have increased. So it is always better to illumine the anger immediately.

When somebody does something wrong to you, try to feel that it is an extended part of your own consciousness that has made this deplorable mistake. Enlarge your heart and feel that it is you yourself who have done wrong. In that way you won't become upset. What you have to do is stop thinking of others and think only of perfecting yourself. That does not mean that you are ignoring the world's problems. No. Your own perfection will help others. When you achieve something, you will see that very thing in a small measure in others. Similarly, if you see something wrong in others, tomorrow you will see that very thing in yourself. And if you see something good in someone else but not in yourself, that particular thing will soon develop in you. If you see a person who is sincere and you are not sincere, just because you are conscious of his sincerity, your own inner sincerity will come to the fore. Your inner being will try to communicate with the sincerity of that particular person and, like a magnet, it will draw sincerity from that person or from the Supreme, who is the Source.

From now on, try to perfect your own nature instead of looking around to see whose imperfections are standing in your way. Pay all attention to your own self-discovery. When you have perfected yourself, you will see that everybody on earth will gain in perfection through you.

Q How can I tell if I am meditating too much?

A If you are meditating too much—that is to say, beyond your capacity—then you will get a kind of tension or pain in the area of the third eye. Also, you may get a haughty attitude. You may feel, "I am so divine and perfect, whereas everyone else is undivine and imperfect." If you are trying to pull down peace, light and bliss from above beyond your capacity, then you may no longer get any joy or satisfaction from your earthly activities. You may come to feel that this earthly existence of yours is useless and meaningless. If you get this kind of disgust or depression which makes you want to withdraw from the world, then you may be trying to meditate beyond your capacity.

Q When I meditate I lose energy and get tired. Is it because I meditate too much?

A No. If you are losing energy while meditating, it means that your meditation is incorrect. If you meditate well, you will gain energy. Meditation is the way to gain infinite energy, light and bliss. But if the particular method you are using is wrong, then you will lose energy instead of gaining it.

Q Is there anything I can do to always have a good meditation?

A It is through gratitude, the gratitude that is inside the heart, not inside the mind, that you can make your meditation excellent. Just for a fleeting second, remember that once upon a time you were the same as your friends and neighbours. Now look at the difference between you. It is like day and night. They may be rich on the material plane, but on the spiritual plane they are totally bankrupt. When you see the difference, automatically a spring of gratitude will well up inside you.

If you can have a drop of gratitude, inside that gratitude you will find a world of new creation. Once the seed has been sown, it starts germinating and grows into a plant. So when you are not getting a good meditation, the best thing is to think of what you were and what you are going to become. Once upon a time you could not even crawl; now you are running in the spiritual life. Once you see the difference, you are bound to have gratitude to the Supreme, for He is the Doer. It is He who has inspired you and acted in and through you. He has inspired you and He has given you the fruit of your action, so naturally your gratitude will come to the fore and you will be able to have a good meditation.

Cry within.
Meditate within. Dive within.
Your inner achievements will far
outweigh your outer imperfections.

Keeping Your Joy

Keeping Your Joy

❦ Guarding Your Inner Wealth

After you have finished meditating, you have to assimilate the result of your meditation into your inner system. Only then does it become a solid, absolutely permanent experience that is inseparably one with your existence. If you enter into a quarrel with someone or get into some unpleasant situation before the peace, light and bliss from your meditation are assimilated, then everything can be lost. Not even an iota will remain. Even by speaking with someone you can lose what you have received during meditation. Someone may come up to you and say, "How are you?" and he may take away all the peace, light and bliss that you have received. That is why you should not talk to anyone immediately after you have had a high meditation, until you have assimilated what you have received. Also, you should not eat immediately after meditation. You can move around or read if you want, but you should not eat a full meal for at least fifteen minutes or a half hour. If you are very hungry, though, it is all right to take a small quantity of milk or juice.

Normally, it takes quite a few hours to assimilate everything that you have received during meditation, and during that period you have to maintain the light that you got. How? Through your inner awareness, and by being careful of how you deal with the outside world. However, sometimes it happens that during your meditation you are receiving and at the same time assimilating. Then, when you stop meditating, it is all assimilated.

137

You can think of assimilation as establishing a lifelong friendship, an eternal friendship, with someone who has come into your life. If peace, light and bliss come into you during meditation and you do not make them your eternal friends, then naturally they will leave you. But if you establish an eternal friendship with them, then your friends will have an opportunity to inspire you, guide you, mould you, shape you and share with you their divine capacities and divine qualities.

Again, you have to know that assimilation is not always what the soul wants. At times the soul is eager to assimilate and keep something for quite a few days before expressing it. At other times the soul wants to reveal and manifest the qualities that it receives during meditation immediately or after only a few hours. This expression can be to others, to the atmosphere or to the Universal Consciousness. The inner wealth is like knowledge. One person may say, "Let me learn a little and teach that small amount." But someone else may say, "No, let me learn as much as I can, and then I will teach others."

Q What qualities are most important for the absorption of light?

A The absorption of light demands absolute sincerity and purity. Anybody who is one hundred percent sincere and pure in his spiritual life can immediately absorb light. The sincerity that I am speaking of is not ordinary human sincerity, but spiritual sincerity, which is infinitely more subtle. Spiritual sincerity asks whether you are ready to make all sacrifices in order to please God. If God asks you to give up everything for

His sake, if He says, "Give up everything and walk with Me, run with Me," and you are ready to do it, that is called true spiritual sincerity. Spiritual sincerity is constant inner and outer sacrifice. If there is no sacrifice in the inner life or the outer life, then sincerity cannot take birth. Constant self-sacrifice to realise the Highest is called real sincerity.

But if there is no purity, immediately you will lose the light that you have received. Purity is actually the vessel inside you which holds spiritual light, peace, bliss and power. Very often you receive things and then you lose them because impurity enters into you. Impurity does not only have to do with lower vital movements. Doubt, fear, jealousy and insecurity are all forms of impurity. One of the undivine qualities that goes hand-in-hand with impurity is self-deception, so you have to be very careful. If you want to expedite your spiritual journey, then purity must come first. Otherwise, no matter how much light you have received or are going to receive, you will not be able to keep it.

 Each conscious step of purity is a precious milestone-victory along my heart's aspiration-road.

Q At the end of meditation I feel very good. Is there anything I should do with that feeling, or any way to utilise it?

A Whatever you feel should be preserved. How can you preserve it? By offering gratitude to the Inner Pilot. Also, you can try to feel that whatever you have achieved can be transcended. If you have received or achieved a dollar's worth of peace, then next time you can try to get ten dollars' worth of peace. And if you feel that you have developed an inner muscle to receive, then you can continue strengthening that muscle. In this way you can develop a very powerful inner capacity.

Q After we stop meditating, how can we maintain the level of consciousness that we reached during our meditation?

A Here in the meditation hall we are all aspiring; that is why our consciousness is elevated. When we go home, our consciousness will go down. Some calamity may take place or we will just enter into ordinary activities, and we will lose our aspiration. Even if there is no outer disturbance, still we find it difficult to remain in our highest consciousness because we are not used to living there. We aspire for half an hour with utmost sincerity, and then relaxation starts. We feel that we have worked very hard, so now we are entitled to take rest for an hour or two. We do not value what we have achieved. We feel, "even if I lose it, I will get it back tomorrow." So we start reading a newspaper or watching television, and in this way we enter into relaxation.

If we want to maintain the height of our aspiration, then our aspiration has to flow continuously. Suppose we have meditated for an hour or so and we do not have the capacity to continue meditating. Still, we can do something which will maintain and preserve our meditation. We can read spiritual books, sing spiritual songs or listen to soulful music. We can go to visit a spiritual friend or, if that is not possible, call him on the phone and speak about spiritual matters. Another thing we can do is write about our experiences, not with the thought of publishing them but just to keep them in our consciousness. While we are writing down an experience, we are revealing our own inner light. Then, each time we read about one of our own experiences, we get new inspiration and aspiration. Even while we are eating we can remember what experiences we had during our morning meditation. Like charging a battery, we are charging our memory with spiritual energy. In this way we can remain in the spiritual flow that we had during our meditation, and keep our consciousness high until our next meditation.

If we want to maintain our height and make the utmost progress, we have to be very wise in our day-to-day lives in how we spend each second. A time will come when we will not have to have any restrictions in our life; our life itself will be a continuous flow of aspiration. But now we have to use our conscious mind in order to aspire.

 Now is the time to make good use of time. Today is the day to begin a perfect day.

Q Sometimes after meditation I lose the joy that I have received from my meditation, and I feel very bad. Why do I lose my joy?

A There are two reasons why you lose your joy. One reason is that your mind starts functioning most powerfully and vehemently. While functioning in this way, it allows obscure, impure and undivine thoughts to come in either consciously or unconsciously. When impurity enters, joy has to disappear. But if purity is well-established in the mind, the joy will last for a long time.

Another reason why you lose your joy is that your inner vessel is small, and you have taken light, which is joy itself, beyond your capacity. The quantity of light that you have received during your meditation has satisfied you, but your inner vessel is not large enough to hold it. When you lose it, you feel sad.

Q Sometimes I feel very sad when I come down from meditation.

A The sadness that you feel is quite natural, because you were in a higher world and then you had to come back to the earthly level. At that time, the worries and problems of the world enter into you. But if you meditate sincerely for a few years, these problems will not stand in your way, because when you come down from your meditation, you will have tremendous peace, poise, joy and love for humanity.

Right now you have boundless love for your child. But after you have meditated for a few years, you will have even more love for your child, because you will feel the presence of God inside him. Right now you do not feel the presence of God inside your child all the time. If he is naughty or if he breaks something, then you do not think that God is operating inside him. At that time you are exasperated and you say, "No, no, this is not God; this is the devil incarnate." But there will come a time when you will see God inside your son all the time, no matter what he does or what he says. When you progress to that point, you will not feel drained when you come down from your meditation. On the contrary, even when you enter into the activities of ordinary life you will be able to maintain the same joy, delight, peace and poise.

When you are meditating you have to feel that you are climbing a tree. You are going up high, higher, highest to collect the mangoes and bring them down for distribution. But if you feel sad when you come down, that means you want to eat them all by yourself at the top of the tree. You don't want to bring them down and share them with others. So when you go up, always go up with joy; and when you come down, also come down with joy. When you go up, feel that it is for achievement of the highest; and when you come down from meditation, feel that it is for distribution.

If you want to see the Face of God, then you must at least spend some time every day with His chosen instrument: your own heart.

Your Daily Meditation:
Food for the Soul

Chapter 13
Your Daily Meditation:
Food for the Soul

❦ An Appointment with God

If you are serious about your spiritual life, then you have to meditate at least once a day. If you are very enthusiastic, you can meditate three times a day—early in the morning, at noon or during your lunch hour, and in the evening. Your morning and evening meditations can be for a longer time, for fifteen minutes or half an hour, whereas your noon meditation can be as short as five or ten minutes. If it is not possible to feed your soul three times a day, then please feed it at least once. Feel that the soul is a little divine child. If you don't feed the divine child within you, it will not be able to grow and manifest your inner divine qualities and your soul's possibilities.

It is better to meditate well just once a day in the morning than to sit five or six times a day with your eyes closed and just have pleasant thoughts drifting through your head. Each time you meditate you have to feel that you are offering your life-breath to the Supreme and bringing to the fore your soul's light. Only then is your meditation worthwhile. If you feel that you can meditate soulfully only once, early in the morning, then that is enough. You have to see your real capacity, sincerity, willingness and joy. If inspiration is there, that means that you have received the sanction from the Supreme, and you will run very fast. Some people meditate during their lunch hour or when they have a coffee break in the office. That is excellent. But please meditate first thing in the morning also. If you start by doing the right thing early in the morning, then you will be inspired all day.

Morning meditation is best
If you meditate in the morning, you will find that your meditation will be most fruitful. Before the sun rises, the earth-consciousness is not yet agitated. The world has not yet entered into its daily turmoil. Nature is calm and quiet and will help you meditate. When nature is fast asleep, the animal in us or our unillumined consciousness also sleeps. At that time we are still in the world of energising and fulfilling dreams, from which reality can grow. That is why the awakened aspiring consciousness can get the most out of early morning meditation.

Once the day dawns, Mother-Earth becomes divinely energetic or undivinely restless. Especially in the West, because of its present dynamic nature, there is some feeling of irritation in the cosmos or in the outer nature. These restless qualities of the world do not have to enter into you, but usually they will. When people move around, immediately their vibration enters into you, no matter where you are. The air, the light, everything around you becomes permeated with the vibration of human activity and human anxieties. The world is standing in front of you like a roaring lion. How can you enter into your highest meditation in front of a roaring lion? But if you can meditate before the world awakens, when the cosmos is still and people around you are taking rest, then you will be able to have a deeper meditation.

Meditating during the day is very difficult. In the evening, meditation is also a little difficult, because for eight or ten hours you have been in the hustle and bustle of the world. During the day you have met with many unaspiring people, and unconsciously their undivine thoughts and impure ideas have entered into you. So unless you are inwardly very strong, you will have assimilated many unaspiring and uninspiring forces from the world. Therefore, it becomes very difficult to meditate in the evening with the same hope and freshness. If you take a shower before meditating, it will help. If you associate with spiritual people, it will also help.

In the morning all these undivine forces and experiences are out of your memory, at least for a while. During the time that you sleep, all the impurities that have come into you from others are washed away. During the hours that you are sleeping, your soul, like a divine thief, is silently observing you. An ordinary thief will steal something from you, but this divine thief will only give and give. If you need peace at one place, your soul will put peace there. The soul acts like a mother, who comes into the child's room in secrecy, early in the morning, to prepare for him the things he will need during the day. At night while you are sleeping, the soul gets the opportunity to do what is necessary for you. But during the day, when you are absorbed in the activities of the outer world, it is extremely difficult for the soul to give and for you to receive. For all these reasons morning meditation is the best.

 Beauty came to me like the morning rose.
Duty came to me like the morning sun.
Divinity came to me like the morning aspiration.

Evening meditation

If you cannot meditate in the morning, the evening is the next best time, because in the evening at least the atmosphere is becoming calm and peaceful. At noon nature is wild and restless, so your meditation may not be very deep or intense. But in the evening nature is preparing to rest and it does not disturb you. When you meditate in the evening, you can look at the setting sun and try to feel that you have become totally one with cosmic nature. You can feel that you have played your part during the day most satisfactorily and, like the sun, you are going to retire.

In the evening you are tired, and you feel that the whole world is also tired. But there is a slight difference between the world's approach to the truth and your approach. When the world is tired, it will not aspire. It wants only to rest. But you feel that your tiredness can be overcome by bringing more light and energy into your system. When you pray and meditate, at that time new life and new energy enter into you and refresh you.

A fixed time is important

Whether you meditate in the morning or the evening, it is of paramount importance to have a fixed time for your meditation. Even an infant will cry for his mother's milk at a fixed hour. If you own a store, if you always open the door at nine o'clock, then others will have confidence that they can come at nine o'clock and you will really be open. Everything has its own hour. Your inner being and your Inner Pilot, the Supreme, always observe. If you stick to a particular hour, then the Supreme has confidence in you. The Supreme says, "At this hour he is not loitering around; he is meditating. If I offer him something at this hour, he will definitely be there to receive it."

You and God should agree to a certain hour for your daily meeting. When He comes at that hour, if you are fast asleep, He will forgive you. If you are not there tomorrow, again you will be forgiven. But you will not be able to excuse yourself. Your oneness with God will not allow you to forgive yourself. Your soul will cause you such pangs that you will feel miserable. Your soul's love for the Highest is very important to you. When your Eternal Friend is coming, the host wants to be ready. The human mind is a very treacherous thing. Left to itself, the ignorant, obscure mind will try to prevent you from doing the spiritually correct thing. It will find many excuses to keep you from fulfilling your soul's wish. But if your aspiration is sincere and intense, the discipline of having a set time to meditate will help you fight against the lethargy and waywardness of the mind.

When you don't give countless outer things your attention, you will see that truth is looking right at you and giving you the strength to discipline your life.

Suppose you want to meditate at six-thirty. This is your chosen hour. If you get up at seven, your own lethargy and idleness will take away all your inspiration. On the one hand, your lethargy will try to justify itself. It will enter into your conscious mind and say, "Oh, I came home very late; that is why I could not get up." Or, "For the last six days I got up at six-thirty. Since God is all kindness, today He will forgive me." There are so many ways your mind can justify getting up late. But even if you came home late, that doesn't mean that you won't do first things first. The first thing is meditation; the first thing is God.

Once you start your journey, if you do not keep moving toward your goal, then you are lost. You may think, "Today I am tired, so I will stop here and rest. Tomorrow again I will go on." But you have to know that ignorance is more alert than your own aspiration. Once you start justifying yourself, there is no end to it. Regularity will tell you that the goal is real. But if you are punctual, immediately a kind of dynamism and movement is there. Your regularity is like a motor. Because you have a motor, you know that at any time you can drive. Punctuality is when you actually turn the key and start the motor. With regularity you get only a vague idea that you will do it. But with punctuality, you actually do it.

If you are regular and punctual in your meditation, you will notice your own progress. If you can meditate sincerely and soulfully at a fixed hour every day, a time will come when you will become an expert. At that time, you will be able to meditate while doing anything, and you won't need a fixed hour. Eventually you will be able to meditate twenty-four hours a day even though you are talking to people and doing your multifarious daily activities. But for that you need many years—perhaps many lifetimes—of practice.

 No path can be too hard for you if you have one God-gift: faith in yourself.

Q How can anyone find time to meditate in the course of a busy day?

A We have twenty-four hours at our disposal, and we find time to do all kinds of things during the day. What prevents us from thinking of God for five or ten minutes a day? We have time to eat, we have time to sleep, we have time to mix with our friends, read the newspaper or watch television. We have time to do whatever we consider necessary. So when it is a matter of God, how can we say that we don't have time?

God is crying for us to think of Him. If we really care to please Him, we will find the time to think of Him and meditate on Him. But if we don't consider God important in our life, then we will always be too busy.

Q Is there a certain hour in the morning that is most conducive to meditation?

A The very best time to meditate is between three and four o'clock in the morning. This is the *Brahma Muhurta,* the Hour of God. No matter what your standard is, even if you are a complete beginner, you will encounter very little resistance if you meditate at this time.

The Westerner who goes to bed at twelve o'clock or one o'clock cannot expect to be able to meditate at three or four o'clock. If you want to meditate at four o'clock, you should go to bed by nine or ten the previous evening. For someone who has just entered into the spiritual life, seven or eight hours of sleep is essential. If you start sleeping only three or four hours just so that you can get up at four o'clock, it will tell upon your health. Spiritually you will derive no benefit, because you will not be able to meditate properly when you are exhausted, and the body will stand as an obstacle to your inner progress. After you make some progress in the spiritual life, then gradually you can reduce your hours of sleep. When your physical consciousness starts receiving light from above, its need for sleep diminishes.

For most people in the West, the best time to meditate is as soon as possible after you get up, before you start your daily activities. If possible you should try to meditate before seven o'clock. Before the outer world attacks you or demands anything from you, you should enter into the inner world with the idea of nourishing yourself. In this way, you are performing your inner duty before you become involved in outer activities. If you put God first in your life, then everything else will gain a more spiritual perspective. If you can please the dearest in you, who is God, before you enter into your earthly activities, then naturally you are doing the right thing.

Q Should we try to get up spontaneously to meditate or should we set an alarm?

A You should use an alarm. To get the special Grace to wake up spontaneously, you have to be a Yogi. But please, when you meditate, do not keep a clock in front of you. If you really want to meditate soulfully, just dive deep within. When you meditate, you are pleasing the Supreme. He will make you conscious of the fact that it is time to go to school or to the office. If you are really meditating, He will do this. But if you are in the sleep world, dreaming and wasting your precious time, it will not be His responsibility.

Q If you stayed up very late the previous night and are very tired when your alarm goes off, is it better to sleep longer and meditate after your accustomed time?

A You have to know how often you do it. If you are doing it every week, this is not good. But once in a blue moon it is all right. In school you study for months, and then you get a holiday. But if you want to take a holiday every day, then how will you make progress? If you have meditated for months at a particular hour and one morning you are exceptionally tired, all right. But if you go to school at a different hour every day, then how can the teacher be pleased?

Opportunities do not come every day in your life. Spirituality is like an opportunity. If you miss one meditation, you have to feel that you have really missed something, that you have travelled one step less than you could have. When you do not meditate regularly, your consciousness loses some of its capacity, and the road becomes very long. Once you relax, ignorance covers you. If you fail to get up once, then on that day ignorance has conquered you.

Suppose you go to bed at three o'clock, and when it is time for meditation you are not able to get up. But who asked you to go to bed at three o'clock? You will say it was unavoidable; you had to do something most important. But while you are up late doing that important thing, please make yourself feel that at six o'clock there also will be something unavoidable and important that you will have to do: you will have to get up to meditate. If the thing that you did late at night was so important that you could not avoid it, then I wish to say that your meditation is infinitely more important; nothing can be more important than meditation.

Sometimes our fatigue is real; sometimes it is all mental. Even if you sleep for ten hours, sometimes you feel extremely tired. Many people sleep much more than they actually need to. Often it is your mind that makes you feel you are tired and exhausted. The mind is so clever. It will make you feel that if you can sleep for only five minutes more, then you will feel much better. If you are supposed to get up at six o'clock, the mind will tell you that if your body can sleep one minute more, then you will feel better. But if you give that one minute to the body, immediately the mind will ask for five or ten minutes more, and before long it will be seven or eight o'clock. So the best thing is not to listen to the mind at all.

Q Is it bad to go back to sleep after meditating in the morning?

A If you go back to sleep and do not get up until eight or nine o'clock, then your own vital forces or the aggression of the earth, which is agitated at that hour, can enter into the result of the meditation which you did earlier, and ruin it. So it is infinitely better if you can do some other spiritual activity like reading spiritual books or singing spiritual songs.

Q If you set a time for your meditation and are able to get up earlier, should you still keep your original time?

A Yes. If your time to meditate is five-thirty in the morning, at that hour your soul will knock at your door, so you should be prepared. Choose the time that you feel is best, and stick to it. If you want, you can get up half an hour earlier in order to shower and get ready, but then you should start to meditate at your appointed time.

Q For a six o'clock meditation, will we do better if we get up at five and are up for a full hour before meditating? If we enter into activity, will we become more awake?

A It is not good if there is too much activity. If you touch a material object, immediately the consciousness of that object enters into you. If you touch a novel, immediately the consciousness of the author will enter into you. If you are drowsy and start doing housework to wake yourself up, then the housework consciousness will enter into you. If you are drowsy, it is best to take a shower. Water signifies consciousness. Once consciousness enters into you, you will not sleep. So do not enter into any activity before meditation. Just take a shower and then meditate. You can prepare yourself inwardly by reading spiritual writings for a few minutes or by singing some soulful, spiritual songs. But you should not do housework or office work.

Q If we tend to feel sleepy, is it all right to exercise before our morning meditation?

A Certainly. Doing a few exercises can make you feel more alert. It is fine to do a few minutes of hatha yoga exercises before beginning meditation.

Q What should we do if we miss our appointed hour for meditation? Should we try to make up for it at our next meditation by meditating for a longer time?

A If you have to miss your appointed hour one day due to unavoidable circumstances, do not feel miserable. As long as you have not let the hour go by out of inertia or negligence or the feeling that because you have meditated for a few days, now you deserve a rest, then you have not committed a spiritual crime. But you cannot "make up" a missed meditation by meditating longer the next time. You eat three times a day. Suppose that early in the morning you did not have breakfast, and at noon you also missed your lunch. When it is time for dinner, if you try to eat all that you have not eaten in the morning and at noon, it will only upset your stomach. If you do not eat for two or three days, and then you try to make up for the food that you missed during your fast, you will run into trouble.

With meditation it is the same. You have the inner capacity to meditate for a certain amount of time early in the morning, at noon, in the evening or at night. If you cannot follow this routine on a certain day, it is better just to meditate most soulfully at your regular hour. If you try to increase the length of time, if you try to meditate for two or three hours instead of half an hour, your physical mind will not be able to bear the pressure. Instead of creating more capacity, this will break your capacity. It will create tremendous tension in your aspiration-life. Everything has to be done systematically and gradually. Eventually you will be able to meditate for eight hours or ten hours at a stretch, but right now it is not possible.

If your aspiration is really intense, if God really comes first in your life, then you can easily adjust your outer life to make time to meditate. The inner aspiration has infinitely more power than outer obstacles. If you utilise your inner strength, then circumstances have to surrender to your aspiration. If you really want to meditate every day, then I wish to tell you that your inner aspiration will give you the power to do it. Outer obstacles can easily be overcome, because the inner life is the living expression of the infinite power. Before the infinite power, outer obstacles have to surrender.

 A spiritually established life is not an easy task. But a materially satisfied life is an impossible task.

Q How long should I meditate? Is fifteen minutes enough, or should I try to meditate longer?

A It depends on the individual. If you are able to meditate for more than fifteen minutes, do so. But it has to be absolutely sincere and soulful. To sit for an hour just to make yourself feel that you are an advanced seeker will be a mistake. The soul will not be there. You may meditate for five hours, but the meditation will not give you any joy. It will not be fruitful at all. You will only give yourself a headache. If a person can meditate for fifteen minutes most soulfully, and after that, if he feels that he has the capacity to continue, then he can continue. But if he doesn't have the capacity, then it will be a waste of time.

The best thing is to meditate for as long as you can without creating any mental tension. It depends entirely on your capacity. Increasing your spiritual capacity is like developing a muscle. Today you may exercise and become tired after five minutes. After two months you may be able to exercise for half an hour or even more, because you have developed your muscles. There is also a spiritual muscle, which is aspiration. How long and how sincerely you can cry for God depends on the strength of your inner muscle.

Q If I meditate too little, I don't have spiritual energy throughout the day. If I meditate too long, I can't maintain my aspiration.

A The problem is that you are going to extremes. Sometimes you overeat and you cannot digest what you have eaten; sometimes you don't eat at all and you feel weak. When you don't meditate enough you feel miserable, and when you meditate beyond your capacity you feel worn out. But you don't have to pull or push. You only have to discover how much capacity you have. If you meditate for only five minutes, then naturally you will not be inspired throughout the day; but if you meditate for an hour or two, you will strain your capacity, and your body will revolt. So meditate devotedly and soulfully for twenty minutes in the morning and twenty minutes in the evening, and in the afternoon if you have a chance you can meditate for five or ten minutes more. That will be ample in your particular case.

Q Why would the body revolt?

A If the physical consciousness is not powerful enough or pure enough to hold the peace, light and bliss that the psychic consciousness is receiving from above, then it will suffer. If we pull beyond our capacity, we will only break our vessel. Here capacity means receptivity. If we develop great receptivity, then no matter how much we bring down from above, we will be able to assimilate it. That is why I always advise people not to push or pull. We have to accept our life as it is and then try to transform it—not by hook or by crook, but gradually, through aspiration.

 There is a lotus deep within you, but it blooms only one petal at a time.

Q During your meditation if you feel really inspired, can you increase the length of time that you meditate?

A In the beginning it is better just to remain in a meditative mood and read spiritual writings or sing devotional songs. If you have been meditating for half an hour, then after two or three months you can increase the length of time, but do not increase it suddenly. Even if you are inspired, please increase your meditation time by degrees. Otherwise, if today you are meditating well and all of a sudden you double your meditation time, then in a subtle way pride will enter into you. You will be bloated with pride the whole day, and then the following day this pride will not allow you to meditate at all. You will think that you have received everything from your meditation, so for two weeks you will not even get up.

Meditation is like eating or taking exercise. If one day you eat too much, the next day you will have stomach problems. Or if you have the capacity to do five push-ups and one day you get inspired and do twenty, the following day you will be too sore to do even one. So always increase your capacity slowly; then you will have no difficulty. If you are inspired to meditate longer, increase your time only by two or three minutes. If your inspiration continues to increase, after a month or so your meditation will be ten or fifteen minutes longer.

Q I try to meditate for fifteen minutes a day, but I find that it takes me almost this much time to actually settle down into meditation. What would you suggest?

A If you want to meditate for fifteen minutes, try to set aside half an hour. During that half hour, you will spend some time in preparation, which is necessary if you are to have fifteen minutes of good meditation. Some people may find that they do not need fifteen minutes extra. Once they start, they can run. They do not have to take a few preliminary starts. But if it is necessary for you, then take a few practice starts. If it is not necessary, right from the beginning you can enter into your soulful meditation.

Q Today I couldn't meditate in the morning, but I was able to meditate later in the day. Why was that?

A There could be many reasons. When you tried to meditate in the morning, perhaps you needed or wanted more sleep. You did absolutely the right thing by meditating later. If you had meditated well in the morning, then the time that you spent would have left you totally satisfied. But since you felt you did not meditate properly in the morning, then the best thing was to try again later, which you did.

Q I am a housewife with small children. What advice do you have for me?

A Even a housewife with small children can easily meditate, provided you are willing to do first things first. Early in the morning before your family wakes up and you have to enter into the hustle and bustle of life, you can offer a few minutes to God. If you know that at a particular hour your children will require food or attention from you, then you can easily get up ten minutes earlier.

Then, during the day while you are taking care of your children and working in your house, you have to feel the presence of the living God inside them and all around you. Unfortunately, most people do not do that. They look upon their children and their responsibilities as their possessions and their burdens instead of seeing them as God-given opportunities to love God and to serve God. If you can feel that you love your children precisely because God is inside them, then there will be a spontaneous flow of joy and divine love. At that time your children will also feel that their mother has something special to offer.

So please try to feel that between you and your dear ones there is a bridge, and that bridge is God. You are loving your dear ones precisely because God the eternal Beloved is inside them. You are showing compassion to someone because the eternally compassionate Mother is inside you. In that way you can remain in a soulful and spiritual consciousness even while dealing with your children.

Q Sometimes when I am meditating, I feel peace and light all around me. Then someone calls me from the kitchen or some other place, and I have to stop my meditation. Then I feel frustrated.

A First of all, for your serious meditation you should choose a time when your family is not likely to require your attention. But if somebody calls you during your meditation, do not be upset. Feel that the experience that you had during your meditation was most sublime. Now you have to bring this peace, love or light to the person who has called you or distracted you. If you can do this, instead of frustration you will see the extension of the light that you have received. Then you will feel more joy, because your achievement has expanded.

What you are doing is separating your life of meditation from the world of reality. Instead, try to feel that you are bringing the divinity of your meditation into the situation which is the cause of the disturbance. By extending your meditation in this way, you will see it inside your daily activities. Meditation is not only in silence but also in the hustle and bustle of the world. You will find that you can maintain a high consciousness there also.

Wherever you go, go with inspiration and aspiration. Whatever you do, do with love and concern.

Q When we've been in school all day with unaspiring people and we're in an undivine mood, how can we get rid of this mood in order to meditate well?

A Try to think that there are two rooms before you. During the day, when you were with unaspiring people, you were in the unlit room. While you were there, feel that you were caught by some hooligans who were trying to strangle you. They were trying to take away your life—your life of aspiration.

Then, when you sit down to meditate, feel that you have now escaped from that world of destruction. You could have been killed by those forces, but you have escaped into the room of peace, light and delight, which is your true home. When you have that kind of feeling, great relief and gratitude enters into you, and your existence is automatically separated from the world of unreality.

If you do not separate yourself from this world of destruction when you come to meditate, these unaspiring forces will also come. You will carry the vibration, atmosphere and thoughts from that world in your mind. It is as though somebody has thrown a heavy load onto you. You don't know who has thrown it; you are just carrying the load. So as soon as you enter into the other room, just throw the heavy bags away.

Some people take meditation as part of their schedule. They feel that one thing follows another in a continuous series: at eight o'clock they go to the office; at five o'clock they come back; at six o'clock they meditate. But it is wrong to take meditation as just another obligation. Do not unite the uninspiring incidents in your life with the fulfilling incidents. Just separate them and give importance where it is due. When you enter into the meditation room, feel that now you are entering into the real life, whereas previously you were living the unreal life. The moment you do this, you will see that the real life is welcoming you with all its inner wealth.

Q Very often I feel full of love and joy before I fall asleep, and I may remain awake without any conscious thoughts except gratitude. But I am worried about getting up in the morning. I want to be rested.

A If you cannot fall asleep but undivine thoughts are not bothering you, why not try to meditate again? If you do not feel like meditating, then you can read some spiritual books. If it is your bedtime, but you are not sleepy, then the best thing is for you to feel that God has given you an opportunity to meditate more. If you feel sleepy while you are meditating, then you can go to bed. But, if sleepiness is not bothering you, then you should feel fortunate that you can use this time for a divine purpose.

Q Could one make spiritual progress by having a week of solid meditation?

A Then more mental asylums would have to be opened. It is not possible. Only spiritual Masters can meditate for hours and days on end. Ordinary seekers have to talk and mix with people and engage in outer activities. Otherwise, the mind and nerves become very agitated. Then anger comes forward, and also a kind of subtle pride that you have been extremely spiritual for a whole week. Then the seeker becomes abnormal.

Meditating for eighteen or twenty hours a day is possible, but only when you are on the verge of realisation or after you realise God. At that time you will have acquired the capacity. But now if you try it, you will only go crazy.

Do you need happiness? Then do just three things: Meditate regularly. Smile soulfully. Love untiringly.

Keep trying! It so often happens that the last key opens the door. Likewise, it is your last prayer that may grant you salvation, and your last meditation that may grant you realisation.

Never Give Up!

Never Give Up!

❦ Cry Like a Child

Successful meditation entirely depends on our inner cry. When a child is hungry, really hungry, he cries. He may be on the first floor and his mother may be on the third floor, but when the mother hears his cry she comes down immediately to feed the child.

Let us take meditation as an inner hunger. If we are really hungry, our Father Supreme will come running no matter where we are crying. If we have intensity and sincerity in our cry, then we begin to make spiritual progress immediately. Otherwise, it can take years and years.

Again, God-realisation is not like instant coffee—something that you will get immediately. God-realisation takes time. If somebody says he will be able to make you realise God overnight, then do not take him seriously. It takes twenty years to get a Master's degree, which is based on outer knowledge. God-realisation, which is infinitely more important and more significant, naturally will take many more years. In no way do I want to discourage anyone. If your inner hunger is sincere, then God will satisfy that hunger.

If we practise concentration and meditation regularly, we are bound to succeed. If we are really sincere, we will reach the goal. But the difficulty is that we may be sincere for one day or for one week, and then we feel that meditation is not meant for us. We want to realise God overnight. We think, "Let me pray for one week, one month, one year." After one year, if we don't real-ise God, we give up. We feel that the spiritual life is not meant for us.

The road to God-realisation is long. Sometimes, while walking along the road you will see beautiful trees with foliage, flowers and fruits. Sometimes you will see that there is only a road, without any beautiful scenery. Sometimes you may feel that you are on an endless road through a barren desert, and that the goal is im-possibly far away. But you cannot give up walking just because the distance seems far, or because you are tired and have no inspiration. You have to be a divine soldier and march on bravely and untiringly. Each day you will travel another mile, and by taking one step at a time eventually you will reach your goal. At that time you will definitely feel that it was worth the struggle.

 *Love the battlefield of life, for joy is always breathing secretly and openly in both your victory and your defeat.*

Q&A

Q What happens if, after meditating for a few months or a few years, you decide you want to take a rest and then continue your journey at a later time?

A In the ordinary life, after you have covered one mile you can remain where you are for a while and take rest before continuing your journey. But in the spiritual life it is not like that. In the spiritual life, once you take rest doubt enters into you, fear enters into you and suspicion enters into you. All kinds of negative forces enter into you and destroy your possibilities. Your potentiality remains the same; eventually you will realise God. But the golden possibilities that you once had are lost. You will fall back to your old ways and be lost in ignorance, and the progress that you made will be destroyed. However, the essence of the progress that you made will remain inside the soul. The essence is never lost, even though in your outer life you cannot use it. The quintessence of the progress that you made will remain inside your heart, and after five or ten years, or in your next incarnation, when you want to meditate again, this quintessence will come to the fore. At that time, if you pray to God most sincerely to enter into the spiritual life again, your previous progress will loom large in your life.

_Q_ How can I maintain my enthusiasm to meditate every day? Some days I feel no inspiration to meditate at all.

_A_ Some days you do not want to meditate because early in the morning you do not renew your love, devotion and surrender to the Eternal Pilot within you. Every day your Eternal Pilot is ready to feed your inner hunger, yet you may not offer Him your gratitude even for a second. If you can feel a flood of gratitude flowing inside you, then easily you can have a wonderful meditation every day.

What should you do if you feel no enthusiasm or inspiration to meditate on a particular day? For a fleeting second remember what you were before you entered into the spiritual life. When you see the difference between what you were and what you are now, automatically a spring of gratitude to the Supreme will well up inside you, for it is He who has inspired you and awakened your inner cry, and it is He who is fulfilling Himself in and through you.

Another thing you can do is to think of a time when you had a most sublime meditation, and consciously dive deep into that experience. Think of its essence—how you were thrilled, how you were jumping with delight. At first you will just be imagining the experience, because you are not actually having that meditation. But if you enter into the world of imagination and stay there for ten or fifteen minutes, power will automatically enter into your meditation and it will bear fruit. Then it will not be imagination at all; you will actually be deep in the world of meditation.

There is something else that you can also do. Try to feel that the dearest in you—either your soul, or your Master, or the Supreme—is very hungry, and that you are in a position to feed your dearest with your meditation. Your soul, your Master and the Supreme are eternally one, but take them as separate individuals. If the dearest in you is starving and you are in a position to feed him, will you not do so? If you really call someone your dearest, your heart will compel you to feed him. After you feed him, he will give you satisfaction, and in that satisfaction you become eternal, infinite and immortal. When the child is hungry, the mother comes running to feed him. After the child is fed, he gives his mother a smile. The mother sees her whole world, the entire universe, inside the smile, because the child is her universe. So, when you feed the dearest and the dearest smiles, at that time you will feel that your entire world is smiling.

Every day you cannot eat the most delicious food. In the spiritual life also, especially in the beginning, it is next to impossible to have a most successful meditation every day. Even spiritual Masters have gone through dry periods in their inner lives. But even if the food is uninspiring, still you eat in order to keep your body fit. When you meditate you are feeding your inner being, the soul. If you cannot feed the soul most delicious food each day, you must not give up trying. It is better to feed the soul something than to allow it to starve.

To maintain your inspiration, each time you sit down to meditate in the morning you have to feel that you are continuing the journey that you have already begun. You should not feel that you are beginning your journey anew. No, you should feel that you have already made considerable progress and that today you will make more progress. And each time you make progress you have to feel that you have touched a tiny portion of the goal. In this way you will feel that you are really advancing.

Even better, you should feel that your goal is not millions of miles away, but very close, right in front of your nose. If you always feel that your goal is within easy reach, but that you don't know where it is, then you will desperately cry for it and search for it. At that time, your inner being will be flooded with dynamism. If you feel that your goal is far, you become relaxed and feel that Eternity is at your disposal. But if you feel that what you want to grow into is just beside you, and that you only have to use your conscious awareness to grasp it and claim it, then you will eagerly jump into your meditation.

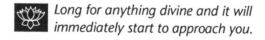 *Long for anything divine and it will immediately start to approach you.*

Only a very advanced seeker can maintain the same level of meditation each day. In the beginning you should be happy if you have a very good meditation even occasionally. When you do not have a good meditation, do not allow yourself to become a victim to frustration, for that will affect your ability to meditate the next day as well. You have to know that God wants your realisation infinitely more than you want it, so your realisation is His responsibility and His problem. If

God has not given you a good meditation today, instead of getting angry or disheartened, try to feel that He is planning to do something more important for you in some other way. If you cannot meditate one day, feel that the Supreme wanted you to have this experience, and just offer your present achievement soulfully and devotedly at His Feet. Say to Him, "These are my possessions right now—unwanted possessions—and I am offering them to You. I place them at Your Feet." If you can offer your existence to the Supreme in that way, then you will see that your daily meditations will become most fruitful.

Q Will I ever reach the point where I will always have the inspiration and aspiration to meditate?

A Right now your meditation is at the mercy of your inspiration or aspiration. When you are inspired, when you have aspiration, you are ready to meditate. Unfortunately this aspiration, this inner urge, lasts only for a day or for a few weeks and then it disappears. But when you become an expert, meditation will be at your command. How can you become an expert? If you want to become an expert singer or poet or dancer, you have to practise daily. It is the same with meditation. If you practise meditation daily, there comes a time when it becomes spontaneous; you develop an inner habit. After a while, at a certain hour you will feel compelled to meditate. You will feel that meditation is your soul's necessity, and the inner urge to meditate will never leave you. Early every morning when it is time for your meditation, your inner being will come and knock at your heart's door. Then you will have a good meditation every day.

Q Why do some people always meditate well?

A In your class at school, I am sure that you are a brilliant student. Again, there are some students in your class who do not do well at all. You are a good student because you study at home. Some of your friends do not study, so they do not do well. In the spiritual life also you have to know that some students meditate without fail every morning, noon and evening. When they meditate with all their heart and soul, God is pleased with them and intensifies their inner cry so that they are able to meditate well every day. Sincere seekers get from God additional capacity, and with that divine capacity they can always meditate well.

 My life of progress is the result of my heart's little cry and my Lord's big Smile.

Q My aspiration seems very feeble, and I'm worried it won't get any stronger in the future.

A Let us not worry about the future. Let us think of the present. As you sow, so you reap. In the past perhaps you have not sown the proper seed. Let us say your inner cry was not intense in the past, and that is why your aspiration is not strong right now. Right now you are not crying for God all the time; you do not have the feeling that without God you cannot exist. You feel that as long as there are interesting things in the world, as long as you have friends, as long as you are comfortable, you can go on. But when you feel that you can exist without water, without air, without everything, but not without God, at that time you can be certain that you will find fulfilment in the future.

If you sow a seed now, it will eventually germinate and become a plant. If we sow the proper seed—that is to say, aspiration—then the aspiration-tree will bear fruit, which we call realisation. But if we do not sow the proper seed inside ourselves, then how can we get the proper fruit? So let us not worry about the future. Let us only do the right thing today, at this moment, here and now. Try to aspire today, and let the future take care of itself.

Q How can I improve my morning meditation?

A Every morning you have to offer your gratitude to God for having awakened your consciousness while others are still sleeping, and for all His infinite blessings to you. If you offer just a fragment of your gratitude, you will feel God's Compassion. Then, when you feel God's Compassion, try to offer yourself. Say, "I will try to please You only in Your own way. So far, I have asked You to please me in my own way, to give me this and that so that I can be happy. But today I am asking for the capacity to please You in Your own way." If you can say this sincerely, automatically your morning meditation will be better.

God is ready to dawn in your mind's chaos, but being a perfect gentleman, He awaits your gracious invitation and precious dedication.

Q How do you feel about collective meditation or group meditation?

A Individual meditation should be done early in the morning at home, when you are alone. But collective meditation also has its time. When you enter into the spiritual life you try to widen your consciousness. If you claim to be a member of a larger spiritual family, then it is your duty to be of service to others. When you meditate with others you can be of real help to them, and they can be of real help to you.

Nobody meditates well every day. Let us say that today you are in a very high state of consciousness, while the person who is sitting beside you is not in his highest consciousness. If both of you are meditating together, your aspiration and even your very presence will inspire and lift up that person. Then, tomorrow it may happen that you are not inspired to go high, whereas the other person is in a high consciousness. At that time he will be able to lift you up. So collective meditation is meant for mutual help.

You have to feel that collective meditation is like a tug-of-war. Suppose that you are in a very high state of consciousness and the seeker beside you is also in a very high state of consciousness. If ten persons meditate together and they are all in a very high state of consciousness, then it is like ten persons on one side in a tug-of-war against ignorance. Since ignorance is only one person, then naturally it will lose the tug-of-war. If you are meditating at home alone and are fighting against ignorance all by yourself, then you may soon become exhausted and give up. But if you can meditate with others, it becomes much easier.

When you meditate in a group, you have to feel your oneness with others. You should not feel that you are competing with anyone else, or that you are stronger or weaker than anyone else. Each individual has to feel that he is strong only by virtue of his oneness with the others. He has to feel that he is strong because he has become one with the aspiration of his brothers and sisters.

During collective meditation try to feel that others are not separate entities. Feel that you are the only person meditating, and that you are entirely responsible for the meditation. When everyone has entered into you, when everyone is flowing in you and through you, at that time you will get the maximum benefit from your collective meditation. If twenty persons are sitting together, they have to feel that they are only one vessel. They are not individuals; they have become one vessel, and they are one in their receptivity. But each one has to feel that it is his obligation and responsibility to do his part. You cannot feel, "Oh, since we are all one, let him meditate for me."

During collective meditation you should have a good feeling for the other persons meditating with you, but do not think of them specifically. If you think of someone in particular, and that person is not aspiring, then your meditation will be on that unaspiring person and not on God. You have to feel that the highest consciousness is the goal, the target, and you are aiming your aspiration-arrow at the target. On the outer plane, if one member of the team scores a goal, that is enough. But in meditation each person has to score. If ten persons can score at the same time, only then does the group get a very high mark.

Q Is there anything wrong with seekers meditating together if they follow different Masters?

A It is not advisable for seekers following one path to meditate with seekers of another path. If you are following one path and the person sitting beside you is following a different path, in spite of your best intentions there will be an inner conflict between your aspiration and his. When you are ready to fly, the person next to you will pull you back. Unconsciously each of you will have the urge to surpass the other. He will try to go beyond you, and you will try to go beyond him. Even if you consciously say, "We are not competing," this does not help. There is an unconscious competition. You feel that your path is better than his, and he feels that his is better than yours.

It is always advisable that the disciples of one spiritual Master meditate only with those on their own path or with those who have not yet chosen a path. It is not that you are being mean; far from it. Only you feel that you live in your house and somebody else lives in his own house.

But when it is a matter of inspiration, if you want to talk with spiritual people who follow other paths, you can. You are trying to reach God, and they are trying to reach God. That means that you and they both possess inspiration. So if you speak with them, you will both get inspiration.

Q What happens if we are meditating next to someone who is thinking worldly thoughts?

A If your meditation is very high, very powerful, at that time inner fire emanates from you. If someone who is cherishing worldly thoughts sits with you, he will be compelled to give up those thoughts. Many times I have seen this when three or four people are meditating together. If one of them is in a very high meditation, then those who are cherishing worldly thoughts either have to leave the place or they are compelled from within to meditate soulfully.

When you are right, everything around you is right, for the beautiful flow that is inside your heart has the capacity to spread its fragrance of oneness-light all around you.

Q How can I maintain the peace that I feel at a group meditation when I get home?

A If you meditate at home every day, then it will be very easy for you to maintain that peace. It is very important to meditate every day without fail. Early in the morning is the best time, before the day dawns. Every day begins with new inspiration, new hope. New life is entering into us every morning, so morning meditation is indispensable for anybody who would like to follow the spiritual path.

Also, if you can mix with spiritual people, they will be able to help you. You will not ignore or hate others; far from it. Spiritual people do not hate mankind, but they have to be cautious. You have to know that your power, your capacity, is very limited. As long as your capacity is very limited, you cannot mix freely with all and sundry. So try to mix with spiritual people and meditate regularly. When you have enough inner strength, then you won't lose anything no matter what you do. Whatever you get from group meditations and whatever you get from your own meditation you will be able to preserve.

Q How can someone achieve the strength to go forward on the spiritual path?

A You have to constantly ask yourself one thing: do you want God or do you want ignorance? Both are standing right in front of you at every moment, and you must make a choice. Everybody knows that one cannot serve two masters. So when these two masters stand in front of you, you have to decide immediately which one you want. If you choose God, then you must come to Him and enter into him. And each time you find that you have come out of a divine consciousness, you have to enter into it again. If you can re-enter into God's Consciousness faithfully and quickly every time you come out of it, then eventually you will reach the point where you will not come out of it and enter into ignorance anymore. A day will come when your conscious choice of God will be permanent, and you will be totally merged in God forever.

As you begin your spiritual journey, always try to feel that you are God's child. Early in the morning you can soulfully repeat, "I am God's child, I am God's child." Immediately you will see that whatever is dark, impure and ugly in you will go away. Later in the day, when ignorance comes to tempt you, you will feel, "I am God's child. How can I do this? I cannot enter into ignorance." By repeating, "I am God's child," you will get abundant inner strength and will power.

When you have the courage to try, you have everything, for God-revealing reality loves you and needs you.

Q How can I always maintain a strong and intense aspiration?

A The mistake that you and others make is that you have a fixed goal. If you come to a certain standard during your meditation, you feel that you have reached your goal. Or if you get a little joy in your inner life, then immediately you get a complacent feeling. You want to rest on yesterday's laurels. But I wish to say that our goal is an ever-transcending goal. Yesterday you got an iota of joy, and today you are crying to get that same iota of joy. But how do you know whether the Supreme wants you to have that iota of joy or whether He wants you go farther, higher and deeper?

In your case it happens that you always try to reach a particular goal. If you know how to run fifty metres, then after you have run fifty metres you feel that your part is over. But the Supreme does not want you to be satisfied with fifty metres. He wants you to run fifty-one, fifty-two, fifty-three, fifty-four metres. When you have a higher goal, automatically your aspiration increases. Otherwise, if you always aim at the same goal, you don't make progress, and it becomes monotonous. If you always go to the same place, after a while you don't want to go there anymore. But if you feel that your goal is constantly farther, higher, deeper, that it is ever-increasing, ever-ascending, then there is constant enthusiasm.

Joy is in progress, not in success. Success ends our journey, but progress has no end. When you have a fixed goal and you reach it, that is your success. After that, you are finished. But if you don't have a fixed goal, if your goal is going higher all the time, then you will constantly make progress, and you will get the greatest satisfaction.

So do not be satisfied with success. Aspire only for progress. Each time you make progress, that is your real success. Every day when you meditate, feel that you will go still deeper, fly still higher. Then you will be able to maintain your intensity and enthusiasm.

Q How can we maintain a good standard consistently, instead of going up and down?

A Please feel that every day is equally important. Your difficulty is that when you do something well you feel that you deserve some relaxation. Today you do a wonderful meditation, and then you feel, "Oh, since today I had a wonderful meditation, tomorrow I can relax." You feel that your meditation will maintain the same speed, but it doesn't.

Every time you meditate, you have to feel that this may be your last chance. Feel that tomorrow you may die, so if you fail today, then zero will be your mark. When the teacher gives you the examination paper today, please don't feel that tomorrow again he will give you the same examination. The past is gone. The future does not exist. There is only the present. Here in the present, either you have to become divine, or else you will remain as undivine as you were yesterday. Since

Never Give Up!

you want to become divine, you should do the right thing here and now. This should be your attitude.

You should make yourself feel that today is the last day for you to achieve everything that you are supposed to achieve. If you fail today, then tomorrow again you have to feel that this is your last day. No matter how many times you fail, you should feel that each day is your last. If you feel that opportunity will come back and knock at your door tomorrow, then today you will not try. You will feel that you don't need to aspire today because you have so many tomorrows. But before those tomorrows come, the aspiration that you have today may be lost.

Do not give up. If you persist, tomorrow's peace will come and feed your mind today, and tomorrow's perfection will come and touch your life today.

As long as your heart remains an ever-mounting aspiration-flame, it makes no difference what your weaknesses are.

Meditation: The Practical Problem-Solver

Meditation: The Practical Problem-Solver

❦ Is Meditation Practical?

We say that somebody is practical when he does the right thing at the right moment in his outer life. He thinks and acts in a specific way so that others will not deceive him and his outer life will run smoothly. But no matter how clever, how sincere or how conscious we are, at times we are at a loss in the outer life. We do not know what to say. We do not know what to do. We do not know how to behave. Or, despite our saying and doing the right thing, everything goes wrong. We do not know how to cope with our outer existence; we cannot manage our lives. We sincerely want to do something or become something, but we cannot do it.

Why does this happen? It happens because our outer capacity is always limited by our limited inner awareness. But if we are practical in the inner life—that is to say, if we pray and meditate—then we will have boundless inner awareness. One who has inner awareness has free access to infinite truth and everlasting joy, and he can easily control his outer life.

The inner life constantly carries the message of truth and God. Where truth is, there is a seed. Let us allow the seed to germinate and become a tree. When the tree bears fruit, we will see the capacity of the inner world being manifested in the outer world. We always grow from within, not from without.

185

No matter what we do or what we say in our outer life, we are not nearing the truth-light. But if we meditate first, and afterwards act and speak, then we are doing and becoming the right thing. The inner life and inner reality must guide the outer life—not the other way around. The life-breath of the outer life has to come from the inner life. The inner reality must enter into the outer life; only then can we be really practical in the outer life.

Q&A

Q Can we answer our own questions through our daily meditations? And if so, how can we tell if the answer really comes from the heart or the soul, as opposed to the mind?

A Any question you have can be answered during your meditation or at the end of your meditation. If you go deep within, you are bound to get an answer. But when you get an answer, you have to determine whether it is coming from the soul or from the mind. If it comes from the heart or the soul, then you will feel a sense of relief and peace. At that time no contradictory thought will come to negate the answer. But if the answer does not come from the heart or the soul, then the mind will come to the fore and contradict the idea you have received.

Messages that come from the mind will have no certainty in them. This moment the mind tells you one thing; the next moment the mind tells you something else. This moment your mind will tell you that I am a very good man; the next moment your mind will say, "No, he is very bad." But the heart always offers the same message. When you sit down to meditate in the morning, it gives one message. In the evening when you meditate, you will get the same message from the heart.

If you get an inner message to see somebody—let us say your boss—you will simply go and see that person. But if the message comes from the mind, before you see him there will be many questions in your mind. Then, if you finally do see him and the result does not come out according to your satisfaction, you will curse yourself and say, "No, it was not the right thing to do. I got the wrong message."

But if the message comes from the soul, you will have tremendous conviction, and you will take both success and failure with equal satisfaction. While you are executing the message, you will not expect anything in your own way; you will not expect that your boss will be pleased with you or will do something for you. You will just do it, and whether the result comes in the form of success or failure, you will feel that you have done the right thing.

Q How can we tell if an inner message is coming from the emotional vital rather than the soul?

A You can take the vital as one runner and the soul as another runner. The vital-runner goes very fast at the beginning, with excessive excitement and enthusiasm, but he does not reach the goal. He runs about thirty metres out of a hundred, and then he cannot run anymore. The soul-runner also runs very fast at the beginning. But once the starter fires the gun, he does not stop until he reaches his goal. The soul knows its capacity and will go to the goal with utmost confidence.

When you get a message, immediately try to see which type of runner is represented. Is this the runner who will stop only when the goal is reached, or is this the runner who will run thirty metres and then lose all his energy? If the message comes from the emotional vital, you will feel that the answer you get will not take you to your goal. But if it comes from the soul, you will feel confident that it will take you to the goal.

Here is another way. When you hear a voice which is offering you a solution to a problem, imagine that a vessel is being filled. If you get the feeling of a vessel being filled slowly and steadily, drop by drop, with utmost inner security, then you will know that it is the soul's voice. Otherwise, you will feel that the vessel is being filled with a tumbler or a glass in a hurried manner. It will fill up quickly, but very soon it will begin to spill over the top. The soul will fill the vessel with utmost confidence and inner poise. If you have that kind of patient feeling, then you can know that it is the soul's voice.

A third way is to imagine a flame inside your heart. There are two types of flames. One is steady; the other is flickering. The steady flame inside your heart is not disturbed by any inner wind. But the flickering flame is disturbed by fear, doubt, anxiety and worry. If you feel that your answer is a flickering flame, then it is the voice of the emotional vital. But if it is a very steady flame rising towards the highest, then you will know that it is the soul's voice. Once you know that it is the soul's voice, you can have utmost confidence in that message.

Q Can one learn to overcome one's fears through meditation?

A Through meditation, outer fear and inner fear are bound to leave us. Now you are a victim to fear because you do not know how to expand your consciousness. But when you take refuge in your divinity, with the help of meditation, then fear has to leave you, for it feels that it is knocking at the wrong door. Now you are helpless, but fear will be helpless the moment it sees that through meditation you are in touch with something most powerful.

The very purpose of meditation is to unite, expand, enlighten and immortalise our consciousness. When we meditate, we enter into our own divinity. Divinity is not afraid of humanity, because divinity has infinite power. When we have free access to divinity, when our entire existence, inner and outer, is surcharged with divinity's boundless and infinite power, then how can we be afraid of humanity? It is impossible!

Q Can meditation protect us from all the injustice we experience in life?

A When you have to defend yourself or protect yourself, always try to use a higher weapon. If people say something and you retaliate on the same level, there will be no end to it. Again, if you simply swallow your anger, they will continue to take advantage of you. But when they see and feel tremendous inner peace in you, which you can get from your meditation, they will see something in you which can never be conquered. They will see a change in you, and this change will not only puzzle them but also threaten and frighten them. They will feel that their weapons are useless.

Peace is the most effective weapon with which to conquer injustice. When you pray and meditate, your whole being becomes flooded with peace. This is not something imaginary. You can feel peace; you can swim in the sea of peace. Then, no matter what other people do, you will feel that they are just children playing in front of you. You will say, "These are all children. What more can I expect from them?" But right now, because they are grown up in terms of years, you become angry and upset instead. If you pray and meditate regularly, you will soon feel that your peace is infinitely stronger, more fulfilling and more energising than the unfortunate situations that others create.

Have no fear. Nobody has any power of his own. Only God has power, and His power is another name for His sleepless Love.

Q Is there a spiritual way to break bad habits?

A Certainly there is. Before you do anything, always meditate for a minute or at least for a few seconds. The power of that meditation will enter into the bad habit like an arrow. Meditation, the soldier, will use his divine arrows against bad habits. This is absolutely the best way.

Q Can meditation help cure physical ailments such as high blood pressure?

A Meditation means conscious awareness of our source. When we meditate, we consciously try to go to the source, which is all perfection. Our source is God, our source is truth, our source is light. Meditation takes us to our source, where there is no imperfection, no ailment. And where is the source? It is within us.

When we meditate, what result do we get in the outer life? We make our mind calm and quiet. It is almost impossible for most human beings to have peace of mind. He who does not have peace of mind is a veritable beggar; he is like a monkey in a human body. He has no satisfaction. But if we get peace of mind for one fleeting second, we feel we have accomplished a lot in life. When we have peace of mind, our vital and our body become peaceful; and where there is peace there is no disharmony. It is only in the world of anxiety, dissatisfaction, tension and confusion that there is disharmony. Otherwise, there would be no ailments.

High blood pressure, heart failure and all the diseases that we notice in God's creation are due to the presence of negative forces. These negative forces can be overcome only when we surrender to the positive force. When we meditate, we try to become a perfect channel for the positive force. The positive force is light, and the negative force is darkness. The positive force is love, not hatred. The positive force is belief, not disbelief. At each moment in our life the positive force helps us because it takes us consciously to our destination, which is perfection.

If our mind is calm and quiet, if our vital is dynamic, if our body is conscious of what it is doing, then we are inside the palace of satisfaction, where there can be no disease, no suffering, no imperfection, no obstruction to our abiding peace, abiding light, abiding satisfaction. Meditation is a means; it is a way; it is a path. If we walk along this path, then we reach our destination, which is all perfection.

Q If we are confused and nervous, how will meditation ever be able to help us?

A In the physical world, when somebody has a headache or a stomach upset, he goes to a doctor and the doctor cures him. If somebody is sick, then how can we say that he will never be well again? If he takes medicine, then there is every possibility that he will be cured. For a sick person, medicine is the answer. If somebody is assailed by anxiety, worry and confusion, meditation is the remedy. Just because he is a victim, we can't say that there will be no saviour. The saviour is there, provided the individual wants to be cured.

Suppose somebody is assailed by confusion and negative forces that deplete all his energy and take all joy out of his life. He is depressed and has surrendered to frustration owing to countless problems in his life. Let us take him as a patient: he needs a doctor, he needs treatment. When an individual is suffering from a few ailments in the mental world, he has to go to someone who has some peace of mind, some light, some inner assurance for him. This is a spiritual teacher. The spiritual teacher is like a doctor who will advise the person as to how he can free himself from fear, doubt, confusion, tension and all the negative forces that are torturing him.

Q Is it really necessary to seek help when we are suffering from mental problems? Can't we just meditate by ourselves and find the answer?

A Suppose you say, "I am suffering from certain mental difficulties, but I know the answer is inside. Now it is all night, but I feel that there is light inside my heart." This is what you feel, but you find it difficult to go deep within and discover the light. Then you have to go to someone who can bring to the fore the light that you have within you. It is as if you have misplaced the key to your own house and you don't know how to open the door. But a friend of yours comes with a light and helps you look for the key. After you find it with his help, you open the door and then he goes away. If you are ready to search in the dark for the key that you have lost, then you can try. But if you have a friend who has a light, then you can have more confidence in finding the key. So the teacher is a helper, an eternal friend who helps you in your search. When he helps you find the key, he won't keep it. He won't say it is his key. No! It is your key, your house, your light. Then you will enter into the house and get everything that you needed and wanted.

Q If we feel nervous or upset, how can we bring down peace?

A There are two ways. One way is to breathe in quietly and say "Supreme" three times very slowly. But if you find this difficult, you can invoke the Supreme as fast as possible. Fear or anxiety has a speed of its own. If you are about to be attacked by your enemy, then try to utter the name of the Supreme much faster than the speed of the attack you are getting from anger or fear. If you can do this, the Supreme will immediately conquer your anger, frustration or fear.

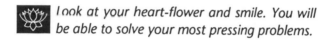 *Look at your heart-flower and smile. You will be able to solve your most pressing problems.*

Q How can one remain calm in the mind when one has so many things to do in so little time?

A First of all, if you are not peaceful, do you think that the things you have to accomplish will be accomplished sooner? No! When you are restless and agitated, when you are full of anxiety and worries, you just add to your problems and difficulties. Suppose you have a destination which you want to reach as soon as possible. If you carry inside you undivine elements like fear, doubt, anxiety, insecurity and so forth, that means you are carrying an extra weight and diminishing your capacity. So how will you reach your goal at the earliest possible hour? Your appointed hour will be delayed.

A runner knows that if he carries extra weight, his opponents will defeat him. You have to feel the necessity of emptying your mind all the time. When doubt, fear, insecurity or any other negative forces enter into your mind, just empty them out, cast them aside so that you can run the fastest. Worries and anxieties will never help us. On the contrary, they will delay us. But if we have peace of mind, then we can run the fastest toward the goal.

Q How can we use meditation to get rid of pain?

A You should try to invoke light in order to cure pain. Pain is, after all, a kind of darkness within us. When the inner light or the light from above starts functioning in the pain itself, then the pain is removed or transformed into joy. Really advanced seekers can actually feel joy in the pain itself. But for that, one has to be very highly advanced. In your case, during your prayer or meditation you should try to bring down light from above and feel that the pain is a darkness within you. If you bring down light, then the pain will either be illumined and transformed or removed from your system.

Q One time when I was meditating I suddenly found myself thinking about some friends who needed some help. I could never describe the power I felt at this time, but I took these friends and lifted them. Two or three days later these friends were helped. Somebody needed a job and he got it, and somebody was ill and he got better. Is it related to my experience or was it mere coincidence?

A It was not a coincidence; far from it. It was your own inner being that helped them. At that time you became the instrument of the Inner Pilot, the Supreme. The Supreme wanted to help those people, and

He actually made you the instrument to help them. It was not a coincidence.

When you meditate and enter into your highest consciousness, your soul automatically tries to help your dear ones. When you enter into a very high, very deep realm of consciousness, automatically the power from within comes to the fore and you can help others. Sometimes your friends do not know who has helped them. But your soul knows and their souls know that the help has come from you. It is not your mental hallucination or ego.

If you can become a better listener, God's Compassion will immediately become a better adviser.

Do not try to change the world. You will fail. Try to love the world. Lo, the world is changed, changed forever.

Meditation in Action: Serving Others

Meditation in Action: Serving Others

❧ How Do I Share My Meditation?

When we meditate in silence with utmost devotion, that is one form of meditation. When we try to dedicate our work to God or to the world, that is another form of meditation, which we may call manifestation. At that time we are serving the divinity in humanity.

In order to serve the divinity in humanity effectively, we have to consciously feel God's presence in those we are serving. While we are speaking to someone, we have to feel that we are speaking to the divinity within that person. Otherwise, if we are just helping someone in our own way without any conscious feeling of dedication to the Supreme, that work cannot be considered as a form of manifestation or as meditation in action.

If we pray and meditate, we will feel that God is inside everybody, that He is a living reality. God is everywhere and in everything, true. But if we pray and meditate, then this mental belief becomes a real, living truth to us. At that time we will consciously serve each person precisely because we know and feel that God is inside him.

If we do not see God, truth, or light in our action, then our physical mind may not be convinced of the value of the things that we are doing. Today we will serve someone and tomorrow we will say, "Oh, he is such a fool! He has no aspiration, no good qualities! Why should I serve him?" If we look at an individual without prayer and meditation, we will separate the person from the soul. But if we pray and meditate, then we will see the soul, the divinity inside each person, and we will try to bring their divinity to the fore.

If we pray and meditate, then our work will be dedicated service, and this dedicated service will help us to make spiritual progress. There are many people who work fifteen, sixteen hours a day. But their action is not dedicated service. They are only working mechanically to make money and take care of their outer responsibilities. But if we really wish to dedicate our life to God and mankind, then prayer and meditation will enable us to do so.

Q&A

Q Should a person shut himself away all alone and reject humanity in order to meditate?

A Humanity is part and parcel of God. By rejecting humanity, how are we going to embrace divinity? We have to accept the world as it is now. If we don't accept a thing, how can we transform it? If a potter does not touch the lump of clay, how is he going to shape it into a pot? He who meditates has to act like a divine hero amidst humanity.

Humanity at present is far, far from perfection. But we are also members of that humanity. How can we discard our brothers and sisters, who are like the limbs of our own body? If we do that we will only limit our own ability to act effectively in the world. We have to accept humanity as our very own. If we are in a position to inspire others, if we are one step ahead, then we have the opportunity to serve divinity in the ones who are following us.

We have to face the world and realise the Highest in the world. We do not want to lead the life of an escapist. Who escapes? He who is afraid, or he who feels that he has done something seriously wrong. We have not done anything wrong and we do not have to be afraid of the world around us. If we are afraid of the world, then we shall be afraid of everything.

Now we see a giant world of imperfection around us. We try to escape it in order to protect ourselves. But I wish to say that a far more formidable enemy than the present-day world is nothing other than our own mind. Even if we go and live in a cave, we cannot escape our mind. We carry that mind with us—a mind which is full of anxiety, jealousy, confusion, doubt, fear and other undivine qualities. This mind of ours forces us to remain in the battlefield of life. If we do not conquer our mind while living in the world, what good will it do us to merely remove our body from the everyday world?

We need not and must not enter into the Himalayan caves in order to meditate. We have to try to transform the face of the world on the strength of our dedication to the divinity in humanity. Meditation is not an escape. Meditation is the acceptance of life in its totality with a view to transforming it for the highest manifestation of the divine Truth here on earth.

Those people who only want to meditate for their own inner peace and progress, and who do not want to offer anything to the world, are selfish. Again, there are those who want to give to the world, but do not want to meditate in order to attain something worth giving. This is foolishness. If we do not possess something, then how are we going to give it? There are many people on earth who are ready to give, but what do they have? So we have to play our part. First we have to achieve, then we have to offer. In this way we can please God and fulfil mankind.

Do you want to change the world? Then change yourself first. Do you want to change yourself? Then remain completely silent inside the silence-sea.

Q Is it possible to maintain the inner peace we feel during our morning meditation throughout the day, especially when our jobs are hectic and we sometimes find ourselves in irritating situations?

A In the morning, when you pray and meditate, feel that you have gained real wealth in the form of peace, light and bliss. As you keep your money inside your wallet, so you can keep your peace, light and bliss inside your heart. With money-power, you can buy whatever you want. Similarly, the spiritual power that you get from prayer and meditation is a real power. When people are quarrelling, fighting or behaving undivinely, just bring forward the inner power which you have kept inside your heart. Peace is power, light is power, bliss is power, just as money is power. Just bring these qualities forward. The power of inner peace is infinitely more solid and concrete than any outer disturbance anybody can create on earth. Your inner peace can easily devour the irritation caused by others.

Q If we meditate well in the morning and acquire some peace, light and bliss that we can keep with us during the day, will this be noticeable to others?

A If you have achieved something in your meditation, your friends and colleagues are bound to see something pleasing, soothing, beautiful, enlightening and illumining in you. Peace, light and bliss have entered through your soul into your physical consciousness. The higher and deeper your meditation and the more you have received, the more your face and outer being will radiate and glow. After you have finished meditating, just go and look in a mirror and you will see the difference between what you are now and what you were an hour ago. This obvious physical difference is due to the fact that your physical consciousness is manifesting the light from your soul. Even as you walk along the street, you will be spreading this light. It is like a perfume that you have inside you. You are not actually using it; you are only keeping it, but it is offering its fragrance. At that time the world of aspiration and even the world of suffering, depression and despair will definitely see something in you. And it will try to follow you—sometimes with reluctance, sometimes with joy, sometimes with greed; but in some way or other it will try to follow you.

You do not have to tell others hundreds of times how meditation has changed your life. Only let them see you on one day when you have meditated well and on another day when you have not had a good meditation. The day that you have meditated well, they will see a tremendous change in you. Your very presence will inspire them.

Q How can I bridge the gap I feel between my spiritual life, which is full of joy, and my life in the office, which is totally unaspiring?

A Spiritual life does not mean that you will always be sitting in meditation with your eyes closed. When you do something in the outer world, if you can feel that you are doing it for God, then everything you do will become a part of your spiritual life. Otherwise, when you are meditating in your room, you will feel that you are doing the right thing, and the rest of the time you will feel miserable. Dedicated work is also a form of meditation.

In the morning the Supreme wants you to enter into your highest and offer your love and devotion to Him and receive His peace, light and blessings. Then He wants you to go to your office and do your dedicated service. In both cases, if you can feel that you are doing something because you have been asked to do it from within, then you will have the greatest joy. You are not the doer; you are only a dedicated instrument serving a higher reality. If you can feel this, then you will get joy no matter what you do. Even if you are doing something mechanical, something intellectual or something which is absolutely uninspiring, you will get the greatest joy because you are serving a higher cause.

You have to know that you can feel God's presence in anything you do. If you can be conscious of God while you are doing something—whether it is cleaning or cooking or working—then you will feel that God has entered into what you are doing. If you can feel God's presence within your activity, then whatever you are doing is with God and for God. If you can keep your consciousness high and maintain peace of mind while working, then your work itself is a true form of meditation.

 Each devoted moment prepares a beautiful sunrise and a fruitful sunset.

Q When people try to help humanity, isn't it partly because of ego?

A For an ordinary person who is not consciously aspiring, trying to help humanity is a positive and progressive ideal, even if it is partly inspired by ego. But those who are consciously aspiring to reach God have a different goal. Their goal is not to help, but to serve humanity—of course, in God's own way.

As spiritual aspirants, we have to know why we are doing something. Were we inspired by God? Were we commissioned by God? If our actions were not inspired by God, if we are not fulfilling God's Will, then the service that we are offering to the world will be full of darkness and imperfection. If we try to help mankind in our own way, we may think that we are serving God, but really we are just aggrandising our own ego. That kind of dedication is no dedication at all for a true spiritual aspirant.

Q What can I do if sometimes I am angry or upset and don't feel like meditating? Is it okay to do selfless service instead?

A Certainly. If your mental agitation has not affected your physical body, at that time, if you feel that you can work devotedly, you should. When you work for the Supreme, at that time you are doing meditation in the physical. You have a body, vital, mind and heart. If you cannot meditate in all parts of your being, then try to meditate in at least one part. But if all the parts of your being—physical, vital, mental and psychic—work together devotedly, then that is the best form of meditation.

Q If we give up our desires and live all the time in the inner world, how will there be any progress in the outer world?

A If you feel that we cannot live all the time in light, that we have to live in darkness for twelve hours and in light for twelve hours, that philosophy is perfectly all right, according to the standard of certain individuals. Someone meditates for one hour, and then goes out and enters into ordinary life. Someone else can meditate for several hours, while there are some people who can meditate all day and night. It is all a matter of necessity. Inner necessity compels one person to meditate for one hour and someone else to meditate for twelve hours or twenty-four hours.

When somebody meditates for an hour, he gets a kind of satisfaction. During that hour, he could have done something totally different, but he did not. He preferred to meditate. He felt that the satisfaction he would get from meditation was more worthwhile than the satisfaction he would get from working or sleeping or whatever else he would have done during that hour. After that hour, perhaps he may want to go back to the worldly life and its kind of satisfaction. It is a question of what kind of satisfaction a person wants and needs.

There are two rooms. One room is unlit and obscure right now; the other room is fully illumined. One person may say that he wants both rooms equally: "I want to remain in the unlit room for twelve hours and in the well-illumined room for twelve hours." So he is most welcome to do that. But somebody else may not feel the necessity of staying in the unlit room at all. He says, "I want to remain only in the room which is illumined."

Yesterday I was clever. That is why I wanted to change the world. Today I am wise. That is why I am changing myself.

Then there is another person who says, "I have remained in the illumined room for twenty-four hours and I have gotten illumination. Now let me go into the other room which is still dark and illumine it with my light." This person has a big heart, so he enters into the dark room to illumine his brothers and sisters who are still in darkness. He was getting satisfaction, abiding satisfaction, in the illumined room, but this was not enough. He will be fully satisfied only when he goes into the dark room and transforms it with his light. So there are some people on earth who have come back into the world of suffering even though they have the perfect capacity to remain eternally in the world of light and delight.

If we can bring the wealth of the inner world into the outer world, then easily we can illumine this world, and this illumination is nothing other than progress. But first we must enter the inner world—the world of light—and receive something ourselves before we can offer it to the outer world. When we can do this, the inner and outer worlds will become united, and the outer world will become fully ready for the inner message. Right now the outer world is not ready, but a day will come when the outer world and the inner world will progress perfectly together.

Q Do both activity and meditation form the essence of your teaching?

A Our philosophy does not negate either the outer life or the inner life. Most human beings negate the inner life. They feel that the inner life is not important as long as their outer life is pleasant. Again, there are a few who think that the outer life is not necessary. They feel that the best thing is to enter into the Himalayan caves and lead a life of solitude, since the outer life is so painful and uninspiring.

We do not believe in living either a life of solitude or an ordinary human life—the so-called modern life that depends on machines and not on the inner reality, the soul. We try to synthesise and harmonise the outer life and the inner life. The outer life is like a beautiful flower and the inner life is its fragrance. If there is no fragrance, then we cannot appreciate the flower. Again, if there is no flower, how can there be any fragrance? So the inner life and the outer life must go together.

The most important thing a spiritual Master does for his spiritual children is to make them consciously aware of something vast and infinite within themselves, which is nothing other than God Himself.

The Guru: Your Private Tutor

The Guru:
Your Private Tutor

❧ What Is a Guru?

Guru is a Sanskrit word which means "he who illumines." The one who offers illumination is called a Guru. According to my own inner realisation I wish to say that there is only one real Guru, and that is the Supreme. No human being is the real Guru. But although the Supreme alone is the real Guru, here on earth we value time. If we find someone who can help us on our journey towards illumination, we take his help, and we may call him our Guru.

A spiritual Master or Guru is like the eldest child in the family, and the seekers are like his younger spiritual brothers and sisters. Spiritual Masters tell and show their younger brothers and sisters where their Father, the Absolute Guru, is.

The real Guru is not in the vast blue skies. He is inside the very depth of our heart. You may ask, "If He is inside our heart, then why is it necessary for us to take help from somebody else to find Him?" Although this invaluable treasure is inside our heart, we cannot see it or feel it, so we need help. A friend of ours, who we call our Guru or spiritual teacher, comes to us and teaches us how to find our own treasure.

It is not obligatory to have a living Guru, but it is certainly advisable. You know that there is a goal, and you want to reach that goal. If you are wise, you will accept help from someone who can show you the easiest, safest and most effective path to the goal. If you want to take hundreds and thousands of years to realise God, having a spiritual Master is not necessary. But if you want to reach the goal as soon as possible, then certainly it is a necessity.

If you have a Master, it facilitates your inner spiritual progress. A spiritual Master is your private tutor in the spiritual life. There is a big difference between a private tutor and an ordinary teacher. An ordinary teacher will look at a student's paper and then give him a mark. He will examine the student and then pass him or fail him. But the private tutor personally encourages and inspires the student at home so that he can pass his examination. At every moment in life's journey, ignorance tries to examine you, but your private tutor will teach you how to pass the examination easily. It is the business of the spiritual teacher to inspire the seeker and increase his aspiration so that he can realise the Highest as soon as possible.

In order to learn anything in this world you need a teacher in the beginning. To learn mathematics you need a teacher. To learn history you need a teacher. It is absurd to feel that for everything else in life you need a teacher, but not for meditation. Why do people go to the university when they can study at home? It is because they feel that they will get expert instruction from people who know the subject well. There have been a few, but very few, real men of knowledge who did not go to any university. Yes, there are exceptions; every rule admits of exceptions. God is in everybody, and if a seeker feels that he does not need human help, he is most welcome to try his capacity alone. But if someone is wise and wants to run toward his goal instead of stumbling or merely walking, then certainly the help of a Guru will be immeasurable.

Right now, perhaps, I am in London. I know that New York exists and that I have to go back there. What do I need to get me there? An airplane and a pilot. In spite of the fact that I know that the plane can take me to New York, I cannot get there without the help of the pilot. Similarly, you know that God exists. You want to reach God through meditation, but someone has to take you there. As the pilot takes me to New York, someone has to take you to the consciousness of God which is deep within you. Someone has to show you how to enter into your own divinity through meditation.

A spiritual Master comes to you with a boat. He says, "Come. If you want to go to the Golden Shore, I will take you. Moreover, once you get into my boat, you can sing on the boat, you can dance, you can even sleep; but I will bring you safely to the Shore." If you say that you do not need anybody's help, if you want to swim across the sea of ignorance alone, then it is up to you. But how many years, or how many incarnations will it take you? And again, after swimming for some time you may become totally exhausted and then you may drown.

Without a Guru, your progress will be very slow and uncertain. You may get high, elevating experiences and not give them adequate significance. Or doubt may enter your mind, and you may think, "I am just an ordinary person, so how can I have that kind of experience? Perhaps I am deluding myself." Or you will tell your friends about your experiences, and they will say, "It is all a mental hallucination!" But if there is someone who knows what the inner reality is, he will be able to assure you that the experiences which you have are absolutely real. The Master encourages the seeker and inspires him. And if the seeker is doing something wrong in his meditation, the Master is in a position to correct him.

Once you complete a course, you no longer need a teacher. If you want to learn how to sing, you go to a singer and learn from him. If you want to be a dancer, you go to a dancer. Once you become a good singer or dancer, you don't have to go to the teacher anymore. In the spiritual life it is the same. You need help in the beginning, but once you become extremely advanced, you will not need anybody's help.

If someone becomes a true disciple of a Master, he does not feel that he and his Guru are two totally different beings. He does not feel that his Guru is at the top of the tree and he is at the foot of the tree. No! He feels that the Guru is his own highest part. He feels that he and the Guru are one, that the Guru is his own highest and most developed part. Therefore, a true disciple does not find any difficulty in surrendering his lowest part to his highest part. It is not beneath his dignity to be a devoted disciple, because he knows that both the highest and the lowest are his very own.

 *He who inspires you is your real teacher.*
He who loves you is your real teacher.
He who forces you is your real teacher.
He who perfects you is your real teacher.
He who treasures you is your real teacher.

Q&A

Q Does each individual have a specific path or are all paths relatively similar?

A All the paths are not the same, although the ultimate goal is the same. There are different roads, but each road leads to the same goal. Each individual needs the guidance of a Master, and each individual has to discover his own path. Then he must follow only one path and one Master who is the leader or guide of that path.

Each individual must necessarily have a path of his own. That doesn't mean that there will not be other seekers on the path. There will be others who will want to follow the same path, but each seeker will follow it in his own way, according to his own inspiration, aspiration, and spiritual development.

Q Is it possible to follow more than one path?

A If you are practising spiritual discipline under the guidance of a Master, it is always advisable to give up your connection with other paths. If you are satisfied with one Master but are still looking for another Master, then you are making a serious mistake. You will not be able to receive what your Master wants to give you, and your spiritual progress will be very slow. Spirituality is not like a school where you have a teacher in each subject: history, geography and so on. No. God-realisation is one subject, and for that subject only one teacher is needed. So for the fastest progress, it is always advisable to find a Master in whom you have the utmost faith and then remain in his boat only. Otherwise, if you have one foot in his boat and another foot in some other boat, you will eventually fall into the water.

Q How does one know whether he is ready for a spiritual path or not?

A When you are hungry you know that you have to eat. Your hunger compels you to eat something. In the inner life also, when you are hungry for peace, light and bliss, at that time you are ready. When you have an inner cry, then you are ready for a spiritual path. When you feel the need, you are ready. If you don't have the need, then you are not ready.

Sometimes it happens that the seeker is ready and the Master is available, but attachment to the ordinary life prevents the seeker from looking sincerely enough. The other day somebody told me that she has been looking for a Master for nineteen or twenty years. I was so surprised, because I was positive that her Master is alive. If she had really been searching sincerely and crying for her Master, then she would have found him. If the aspirant is really sincerely crying for a path, then his path will present itself before him. If he really cries for a spiritual Master, either the Master will come to him or he will be able to go to the Master. No sincere effort ends in vain. If someone makes a sincere effort, then I wish to say that his inner life and outer life are bound to be crowned with success.

What gives life its value
If not its constant cry
For self-transcendence.

Meditating as Sri Chinmoy's Disciple

Chapter 18
Meditating as
Sri Chinmoy's Disciple

❦ Your Own Personal Guide

Each Master has his own way of teaching his students to meditate. I ask my disciples to begin their meditation by repeating the word "Supreme" a few times. The Supreme is our eternal Guru. If you chant *Aum* soulfully, it will also help you. In the spiritual life, gratitude is of paramount importance. Early in the morning when you first begin your meditation, take three very deep slow breaths, and while you are inhaling, offer your soulful gratitude to the Supreme for having awakened you and given you the inner urge to meditate. Out of millions of people on earth, He has chosen you to enter the spiritual life; so naturally you are grateful.

You may say that you do not know how to meditate. But I wish to say that once you become my disciple, once you enter into my spiritual boat, then it is the problem of the boatman to take you to the Golden Shore. After you are safely seated in the boat, you can lie down, you can sing, you can dance, you can do anything. But first you have to enter into the boat. Occasionally I give instructions outwardly to disciples who need it. But to most I do not give individual meditations. Instead, when I accept a disciple I concentrate on his or her soul and give the soul an inner form of meditation. I bring the soul forward, and the soul actually meditates in and through the seeker. The soul also convinces the heart and mind to do the right thing, so that eventually the entire being—body, vital, mind, heart and soul—will be able to properly meditate. When I concentrate on the disciple's soul, the disciple is bound to receive my inner instruction. But if the disciple can consciously create a pure vibration and keep a sincere attitude, then it is easier for his soul to remain at the fore and to receive everything from me.

Individualised meditation

In the ordinary life if ten students come to the same class in school, the teacher gives them all the same lesson. But in the case of a spiritual Master it is different. When he meditates on his disciples, the consciousness that he gives to one will not be the same as what he gives to another.

When I meditate on my disciples, I motivate and inspire each individual according to his acceptance of me and according to his capacity to receive and manifest the light that I am offering him. Out of God's infinite bounty I have the capacity to enter into each person's consciousness and soul to see what that particular individual needs most, and how he wants to manifest the divinity within himself. One individual's soul may want to realise and manifest the truth through divine power. Another individual may want to realise God through love, devotion and surrender. So first I see what the soul wants, and then I can tell the person inwardly, "You follow this method." I may not tell him outwardly, but inwardly I say, "This is the way you have to realise and manifest the truth." Then the soul may take a day, a week or a few months to convince the rest of the being how to meditate. The mind may not understand, but for meditation the mind is not at all necessary.

From time to time I may outwardly tell an individual how to meditate. But the meditation that I give is given in strictest confidence, and it is meant only for that particular individual. If he tells others and they try to use the same method, that will be a serious mistake.

Meditating as Sri Chinmoy's Disciple

Each person must go his own way during meditation because each has a particular role, a special mission on earth, to fulfil. In God's divine Play, each one has been allotted a particular part, and to perform that part one has to meditate according to one's own inner necessity.

If you feel that you are inwardly drawn to me but you have not received an individual meditation, do not worry. The best type of meditation comes when you enter into my consciousness by looking at a picture taken of me when I am in a high meditative conscious-ness. While meditating on my picture you do not have to think of anything. Just try to throw your outer and inner existence into my consciousness with utmost aspiration. If a thought comes to you, whether good or bad, just throw it into my picture. Each time a thought strikes your mind, feel that it is an attack, and let me have the attack. Do not encourage any thought whatso-ever. In this way you can keep your inner vessel abso-lutely empty. If you empty yourself and give me all your thoughts and undivine qualities, then I can fill you with peace, light and bliss.

The Guru accepts

I am ready to accept from my disciples everything that you have and everything that you are. If you only want to give me the good things, that is not right. You should give me both the good and the bad. If you have fear, doubt or any negative thoughts, look at my picture and throw all your obscurity and impurity into me. Do not worry about me. I will throw these negative forces into the Universal Consciousness. But if you hold on to these things, you will only suffer. Today you will have one wrong thought, tomorrow you will have a hundred wrong thoughts and there will be no end. When these negative thoughts enter into your mind, you have to know that you actually become weak. It is as if a heavy burden has been placed on your shoulders; so natu-rally you become tired and exhausted.

How do you throw negative thoughts into me? Let us say that you are jealous of someone. When you are jealous of someone, you are inwardly communicating with that person and offering him your jealous thoughts. In your mind you are formulating thoughts or ideas, and then you are consciously directing them to him. In the same way you can throw these ideas into me instead. The moment you talk to me inwardly, you have to know that you are giving me your thoughts.

When you do your morning meditation, if your sleep was not disturbed and you have not accumulated any mental garbage during the night, then there may be nothing undivine that you have to give me. At that time you can enter into me with joy, love, peace and all divine qualities. When you do this, it is like a child dealing with his own father. A child goes to his father with such joy to give him a penny that he has found in the street. The child could have used the penny to buy candy, but he felt the necessity of giving it to his father instead. And the father is so pleased that his child has given him his own possession that the father gives the child a dollar.

For my disciples, I am your spiritual father. If you give me something good or positive—a little love, a little joy, a little gratitude—then immediately I will give you boundless love, joy and gratitude in return. I will give you immeasurably more than what you have offered me. But if it is something bad that you are giving, then it will enter into my inner ocean and I will take care of it.

Meditating on Sri Chinmoy's picture
When you meditate on my picture and enter into my consciousness, you should not feel that you are entering into a foreign element or a foreign person, but that you are entering into your own highest part, your true self. You have a mother and a father, you have a husband or wife, you have children; now you can add one more person to your family. You have to feel that here

is someone who is your own—not only for this life, but forever. If you feel your oneness with me, if you feel that I am not a foreigner but a member of your own family, then automatically your consciousness, your soul, will try to associate with mine. This very association will be meditation for you.

If you look at a tree, you become one with the consciousness of the tree. If you look at a flower, you become one with the fragrance of the flower. Similarly, if you look at a picture of me in a very high consciousness, you become one with my inner divinity and reality. Sometimes when you see the ocean of light inside me, you may feel that if you enter into the ocean you will be drowned, overpowered, destroyed. At that time light is trying to enter into you and you are trying to hide. But you have to know that divine light will not expose you; it only wants to illumine you. The more light you receive, the sooner you will be illumined.

But if you feel fear, then it is better for you not to try to enter into me. Instead, you should allow me to enter into you. You can say, "Let the ocean of light come into me in a very, very small quantity, or let just a few drops of light enter into me." Your inner progress depends on your strength and receptivity, on how much of my spiritual food you can eat. If you have great inner strength, if you feel that you are strong enough to swim in the sea of light and bliss, then enter into me. Otherwise, let me enter into you. But this is only for seekers who want to follow my path.

Those who are not my disciples may think that it is the height of folly for anyone to meditate on my picture. Perhaps they feel that I am shamelessly proud. But I can assure you, a picture taken of me when I am in a very high consciousness, when I am totally one with the Supreme, does not represent my physical body or human personality. It does not represent Chinmoy Kumar Ghose. When my disciples meditate in front of my picture, they feel that they are meditating not in front of me but in front of their real Guru, who is the Supreme. The Supreme is the eternal Guru—my Guru, your Guru, everybody's Guru. But I represent Him in a personal, accessible way for those who have faith in me, just as there are other Masters who represent the Supreme for their disciples.

So when you meditate on my picture, please do not think of it as a picture of a human being. Think of the achievement and the consciousness that the picture represents. For my disciples, at least, my picture represents someone who has attained oneness with the Highest. If anyone concentrates on my picture with real devotion and aspiration, I have to help him. To serve mankind is the only reason I am here on earth.

Those who are my real disciples should not meditate on anybody's photograph but mine. Your Guru is the farmer. He is constantly cultivating the field, which is your inner life. If you do not allow him to cultivate, if you consciously or unconsciously turn to somebody else, then you are only delaying your own progress. It is not that I will mind if you put up a picture of some god or goddess in your room; I am very fond of the gods and goddesses. But if I am to carry you to the Golden Shore, then you have to be in my boat. For concentration, for meditation, for contemplation, for all inner guidance you should come to me, for you have a direct inner connection with me.

If you have a beautiful picture of a god or goddess, you can use this picture for inspiration. But if you concentrate and meditate on it, you will create tremendous confusion in yourself. One day you will look at this picture and meditate, the following day you will meditate on another goddess, the third day on somebody else and the fourth on me. Then I will be helpless. So I always tell my disciples to approach me inwardly, and I will always help them.

Love, devotion and surrender are the cornerstones of my philosophy because they make up the true sunlit path which can lead the aspirant to the Goal very fast and very safely. If you want to enter into my consciousness while looking at my picture, the best approach is that of love, devotion and surrender. If you offer your heart's love, devotion, and surrender, then you will feel my presence inside your heart. When someone becomes my disciple, he has to feel my presence in his heart and also his own presence inside my heart. When a disciple meditates on my picture, it automatically helps him in concentrating on the heart. And if he concentrates on his heart, then he will find it very easy to enter into his highest consciousness.

Meditation does not only mean sitting in front of your shrine. If you read my writings soulfully, you immediately enter into my consciousness, and entering into my consciousness is the highest form of meditation for those who consider themselves my disciples. Dedicated service is another form of meditation. When you work for me and think of me while working, my consciousness enters into you and your own consciousness is elevated. This is one of the best forms of meditation.

If you want to follow someone else's path, that person may give you different instructions. But this is what I tell my disciples. I am a spiritual teacher, but I am not the only spiritual teacher on earth; there are a few others. If you want to follow my path, I will be able to offer light to your soul. If you study my writings, if you come to our meditation meetings regularly, and if you concentrate on my picture during your own daily meditations, then I will be able to help you in your inner journey. But if you follow someone else's path, then naturally that teacher will teach you how to meditate in his own specific way.

Q&A

Q One of your pictures frightens me.

A A spiritual Master is not an X-ray machine. As soon as you stand in front of an X-ray machine you are totally exposed. When you stand in front of me I also can see everything, but I will be the last person to expose you to anybody or complain about you to the Supreme. If somebody has done something very wrong, then he may be afraid that I shall expose all his inner defects and secret misdeeds. But I am not going to expose you. On the contrary, my compassion—like a mother—will hide your imperfections. When I accept someone as my disciple, I accept all his imperfections as my very own.

So you should never be afraid of me. I am not a tiger or a lion. I am not going to devour you. Never! Even if you feel that you are darkness itself and I am the sun, no harm. The sun which shines within me is the inner sun, which only illumines. It does not expose. If it shines on darkness, it transforms it into light, and then offers this light to the world at large. So there is nothing for you to worry about.

Please, please never be afraid of me. You can be afraid of anything on earth, but do not be afraid of me. I will never harm you in any way. On the contrary, it is my business to transform your imperfections and mould and shape you into your own divinity.

Q My friend is not a disciple, but she has begun to meditate on your picture, and now she feels great fear.

A Very often people say that they are frightened by my picture. But they are not afraid of my picture. It is only a question of whether they are ready to give up certain things. Inwardly they are unwilling to give up their old habits and old life. They look at my picture and feel an ocean of uncertainty, because they are uncertain themselves about whether they really want the spiritual life, and they are afraid of what will happen if they give up their old habits. Your friend's experience may be interpreted in this way.

If one can forget the past and be ready to enter into the new, the ever-new, consciously and wholeheartedly, then one will see that the new also has its own reality— a more fulfilling reality than the past. At that time there is no fear. Fear comes only when one is unwilling to give up one's old life or is uncertain about accepting a new way of life. But usually people are unconscious of the fact that they do not want to give up their old life. Because part of them sincerely wants to be spiritual, they feel embarrassed that they are still cherishing mundane things. They do not want to admit it, even to themselves.

Anything that binds you, unlearn it. Anything that blinds you, unlearn it. Anything that limits you, unlearn it. Anything that awakens you, learn it. Anything that liberates you, learn it. Anything that fulfils you, learn it.

Q When you gaze directly at me during meditation, or when you ask us to come in front of you to meditate, I sometimes get a little nervous or frightened. I'm not sure what you are doing. Could you explain?

A When I look at you during meditation, or when I ask you to sit in front of me and meditate, at that time I am entering into you to observe what your inner and outer being want. I enter into the physical, the vital, the mind, the heart and the soul. If I see that a particular person is crying for peace, then immediately I bring down peace from above. If I see that someone else wants light, then I bring down light. According to the aspiration, necessity and receptivity of each individual seeker, I bring down different spiritual qualities from above.

Sometimes I see that a seeker does not want anything; there is no aspiration at that time. It is not that the seeker has everything; it is just that he does not have the inspiration and aspiration either to draw something from above or to receive something from me. In these seekers I just try to kindle the flame of aspiration.

In some instances you may have a better meditation when I am looking at somebody else than when I am looking at you. While I am looking at someone else, if you are in a high consciousness and you look at me, at that time like a magnet you can pull my light. Although I am looking at somebody else, more of my light can be going to you than to him. On the other hand, while I am concentrating on you, if you are thinking that all the others are now looking at you, or if your mind is counting how many seconds I am looking at you and comparing this with how long I looked at others, then you will receive very little.

Sometimes when I am blessing someone and bringing down the Supreme's infinite Compassion, that person is absolutely unreceptive. But someone who is sitting somewhere else, whose inner being is fully awake and who is most devotedly meditating on the Supreme, is receiving most powerfully. He is taking all the light that I wanted to give to the other person. At this time I am not at all displeased with the person who is receiving my light. If the person to whom I am offering it is not receptive, then naturally if someone else has the capacity, he should take it. Then, when I meditate on that person individually, if he has the capacity to receive still more, I give him more.

But sometimes it happens that when I come to that person, as soon as I look at him and meditate on him, he becomes nervous and receives nothing. Sometimes you feel that you cannot meditate properly when I gaze into your eyes or when I ask you to sit in front of me. You become frightened to death. But why should you be afraid of me? I am not a snake or a tiger. You are afraid of me because you feel that your ignorance will be exposed. Unconsciously you may think, "In the morning I told a lie or did something else wrong, and now Guru will catch me." Or wrong forces may suddenly attack you. Before you saw me, you were fine, but as soon as you stand in front of me, suddenly all the evil thoughts in the world come forward in you. But you have to know that you always had these enemies, only previously you were not aware of them. Now they are coming forward for transformation.

Do not think of me as an X-ray machine which will expose all your inner imperfections to the entire world. Instead, think of me as a mirror that will let you see what you are doing in your spiritual life. When you are in front of me, you will be able to see your own inner reflection. Whatever you have come with will be visible to you. Good thoughts as well as bad thoughts will immediately be reflected. But if you feel afraid and try to hide, or if you try to make me feel that you are this or that, then you are making a serious mistake. I know what you truly are; I know the mark you are going to get. By trying to impress me with your aspiration, you only lose whatever sincerity you have. Even if you come with only one cent of aspiration, give me that one cent with utmost sincerity. If you come with wrong thoughts, feel that these are your enemies, and separate your existence from them. Either you have to reject them and say, "They are not mine," or you have to say,

"Yes, they are mine, but I am giving them to you. These are my possessions, and I am giving you all of my possessions." Then I can take these forces from you. But if you are afraid of being exposed or of receiving what I am giving you, then you will not receive at all.

I have not come into the world to expose you and judge you. I have come only to love you and perfect you. When I look at you and concentrate on you during meditation, do not worry about what I am thinking of you. I am not thinking anything of you. I am only offering you my spiritual love, light and concern. When a child sees his mother coming to him, even if he is covered with dirt and mud, he will not be afraid. He knows that his mother will not slap him or insult him; she will only make him clean again. The moment you think that you have done something wrong—either in your mind or in your actions—feel that my concern to perfect you is infinitely greater than your concern to perfect yourself. Fear comes because you feel that you will be exposed by my light. But if you can feel that my light will only illumine and perfect you, then there will be no fear no matter how close or penetrating the light is.

Another reason you may sometimes become nervous when you meditate in front of me is because you enter into the nervousness and uncertainty of others around you. It is as if you were all students in front of an examiner. Instead of paying attention to your own inner wisdom, you look around to see what page of the textbook the other person is studying. You think that the question will come from the page that he is reading, and you also want to read that particular page. Then you start to become nervous, not because you are trying to read the same passage he is reading, but because the other person himself is nervous. He is reading a passage, but he also feels that perhaps this is not the right passage. When you start to read his passage, you enter into his consciousness and take on his uncertainty and fear.

Q Do you recommend meditating with folded hands?

A Yes, I do recommend it. If you fold your hands soulfully, it will definitely help you meditate better. If you want to increase your devotion, then always you should try to do something on the physical plane so your physical mind will be convinced. When you pray and meditate with folded hands, your reluctant, unwilling and stubborn physical mind and your entire physical being become more devoted. Everything in you becomes one-pointed.

If it is physically tiring and you are in pain, you have to know that this pain is not going to bring you satisfaction. You can pray and meditate and still go into a very high state of consciousness without folding your hands. But if you fold your hands soulfully, it definitely does help your aspiration.

Some people feel that they get ninety-nine dollars from their inner aspiration, but they need one dollar more in order to reach the destined goal. They know that folding their hands may give them that last dollar. If there is something that they can do which will immediately give them that missing dollar, then they will do it. Others feel that they do not need to fold their hands. They feel that by increasing their aspiration they will automatically get the last dollar. They are also right.

Just because so-and-so folds his hands or because you are worried what someone thinks of you, that is no reason to fold your hands. But if you feel that it increases your aspiration and receptivity, you should fold your hands. But if you do it without any spontaneous inner urge, only to impress others, then you are making a deplorable mistake. After a few days or a few months your own sincerity will come forward and make you stop. Again, just because once upon a time you were folding your hands out of deception and now you have realised your folly, that does not mean that you should necessarily stop folding your hands. It is like curiosity. Some people enter into the spiritual life out of curiosity. They do not have sincere inspiration or aspiration, but out of curiosity they come to our meetings and join our activities. Finally they see that their curiosity is getting them nowhere. At that time they stop their life of curiosity and begin to aspire sincerely. So there is no hard and fast rule.

Q Why do you sometimes ask people to look at you when they meditate?

A You are looking at your hands, but your hands will not give you realisation. I am a Master. God-realisation-consciousness is written on my face and in my eyes, not on your fingertips. You will receive much more inspiration from looking at me than from looking anywhere else.

If you can make a conscious contact with my soul, then you can rest assured that my existence on earth will act like your slave. Once anyone makes real contact with my soul and sincerely wants my help, then I am at his or her service forever. But this contact must be transformed into identification, and from identification into oneness. If a seeker can establish oneness between his soul and my soul, then I shall be always responsible for that particular human being. This is my soul's assurance.

If you want guidance, then look up with a pure heart. If you want guidance, then look within with a doubt-freed mind.

Q Sometimes even when I am meditating with you, I like to keep my eyes closed. Is this never a good thing to do?

A When I am meditating in front of my disciples, I always ask them to keep their eyes half open, because one of the ways they can receive from me is through the eyes. Sometimes I am bringing down infinite peace, light and bliss, and distributing it through my eyes. If the disciples can see these divine qualities with their own eyes in my face and in my eyes, then their physical mind will be convinced, and they will be more receptive. What I bring down you can see not only in my eyes but also in my whole face. It is like a glow that radiates around my body. If your eyes are open, then you are bound to see something.

Q When a Master brings down more light or peace than those meditating with him can absorb, what happens to it? Is it all lost?

A It is not all lost. It enters into the earth atmosphere and becomes the earth's possession. When spiritual Masters bring down divine qualities from above, Mother-Earth assimilates them as her own. Then, when someone is aspiring, he will get this peace and light from the earth-consciousness, but he will not know where it is coming from.

Q Since I started meditating with you, I have felt that my consciousness is in a different place, and I just wondered if you could comment on that.

A Since you have been coming here to meditate with us, your consciousness has begun functioning more from your heart than from your mind. Formerly, your consciousness was in the mind. When you stay in the mind, all of life seems like a dry piece of wood. But when you stay in the heart, life is turned into a sea of pure love and bliss. If you can stay there, you will gradually begin to experience a spontaneous feeling of love and oneness with God and God's creation.

 The fulness of life lies in dreaming and manifesting the impossible dreams.

Each experience is a beautiful incident inside my heart. Each experience is a powerful reality inside my soul.

Understanding Your Inner Experiences

Understanding Your Inner Experiences

❦ Fruits on the Path of Meditation

There are many roads leading to the goal. One road may have beautiful flowers on either side, another road may have only a few blossoms, and a third road may have none at all. If three seekers each follow a different road according to their soul's needs and preferences, each of them will eventually reach the goal, having had quite different experiences on their journey.

Each experience is a step towards realisation. Each experience gives you additional confidence in yourself. Each experience encourages you and energises you to march farther, and gives you enormous delight. While having the experience, you may feel the presence of an invisible guide within you, pushing you towards the goal.

Before you get the fruit that you call the goal, you may want to taste many different fruits. But only when you eat the fruit that is your goal do you get full satisfaction. Some seekers feel that they do not want any fruit but the fruit of God-realisation, so spiritual experiences, as such, are not at all necessary for them. If you have the capacity to run very fast, then you need not have thousands of experiences before realising God. Your expanding consciousness, as you grow into God, is itself a solid experience.

When you do have an inner experience, you may not be able to tell whether it is genuine or not. But only if you do not have a Master will this problem arise. If you have a Master, he will immediately be able to tell you whether you are getting fruitful inner experiences or whether you are just deceiving yourself. A spiritual Master can easily tell without the least possible doubt or hesitation.

If you do not have a Master, you can still solve this problem. Just concentrate on your spiritual heart. If the experience you are having is genuine, then you will feel a subtle tingling sensation in your heart, as though an ant were crawling there.

There are also other ways to tell whether your experience is genuine. Try to breathe as slowly and quietly as possible, and feel that you are bringing purity into your system. Feel that purity is entering into you like a thread, and revolving around your navel chakra. At that time, if you concentrate on your experience and you feel that your spiritual heart is not willing to enter into your navel chakra, you will know that your experience is a mere hallucination. But if the heart gladly enters into the navel, then rest assured that your experience is absolutely true and genuine.

Again, when you have an experience, try for a couple of minutes to feel whether you can grow into that experience or not. If you feel that sooner or later you will be able to grow into that experience, then the experience is genuine. But if you feel that reality is something else and that you can never grow into the experience, then that experience is not genuine.

When you have an experience, try to separate your outer life from your inner life. The outer life is the life of human necessity and earthly requirements. The inner life is also a life of necessity, but it is God's necessity, not your necessity—God's requirements, not your requirements. Try to feel whether it is God's necessity that is operating in and through your experience, and whether God needs and wants to fulfil Himself in and through you. If you have that kind of feeling or realisation, then your experience is genuine. Real experience comes only when you sincerely want and need the inner life, and when God needs and wants the inner life in you and through you. If you have come to that understanding, then all your experiences will be true; they have to be true.

Q Do we consciously remember all of our inner experiences?

A In the case of an ordinary seeker, when he has an inner experience, he may not consciously retain it, although the essence remains in his inner life. Even if it is a high experience, after four years or so he may totally forget it, because the ignorance in his life swallows it. He may say, "How can I have had such an experience? If I did have such an experience, how is it that afterwards I did so many wrong things? How is it that I did not meditate and pray? That means it was not such a significant experience." So his doubt devours the experience and eventually he forgets it. But in the case of a realised person, he knows that whatever he saw or felt was absolutely true. Also, he can remember the inner experiences that he had even from previous incarnations, because of his inner vision. But an ordinary seeker, even if he has had only two major experiences in his life, may not remember them at all.

Q How do we know what plane of consciousness we are in during meditation?

A A seeker can be aware of the planes of consciousness only when he is on the verge of realisation. An ordinary aspirant will not be able to know, and also it is not necessary for him to know.

There are seven higher worlds and seven lower worlds. A spiritual Master can easily be in all these fourteen worlds at the same time and see things that are happening in all the worlds. An aspirant can also be in more than one world at a time, but he will not be able to know which worlds they are. Only someone who is advanced in the spiritual life, someone who is about to step onto the highest rung of the spiritual ladder, will be able to see in which plane of consciousness he is staying during his meditation. For realised souls it is very easy.

Your spiritual Master can tell you which plane a particular experience has come from. If he tells you that a particular experience comes from the vital world or the mental world, then in the future when you get a similar experience you will be able to know that it comes from that world.

Q Is it possible to receive something in meditation and not be aware of the experience?

A Sometimes when we receive light, peace or bliss on a higher level of consciousness, the physical mind is not convinced that it has actually received anything. But it is not necessary for the physical consciousness to be aware of what has been received. Light may enter into a higher part of the emotional being and start functioning for a few minutes or a few days or even longer. There it will create a new soil, and eventually it will grow a bumper crop of inner experiences. But it may take a while for these inner experiences to enter into the gross physical consciousness.

If an experience takes place in the physical consciousness, then we can see and feel it with our senses. At that
time, naturally we can rely on our own awareness. But
if the experience is something very subtle, and is taking
place on a higher level of consciousness, we may not
be aware of it. What we are trying to do is to make the
physical mind consciously aware of what is going on in
the other parts of the being. If the physical and the
spiritual in us are simultaneously conscious of what we
are doing, then no matter in which plane of consciousness we are having an experience, we will feel it in our
physical consciousness. Then we will have free access
to all planes of consciousness, and the physical will not
be able to doubt the reality of these subtle experiences.
Otherwise, it may happen that when the Highest
knocks at the door of the physical, the physical will
deny it.

Q Sometimes when I meditate I feel that I am about
to go through some experience, but nothing happens. What is the cause of that?

A The reason nothing happens is that you have not
reached the height. You are just on the verge of it,
but you do not quite reach it. It is like lighting a stove.
When you turn on the gas, you have to turn the handle
to a certain point before the flame comes. You come
almost to that point, but you stop too soon. If you had
turned the handle just a fraction of an inch farther, you
would have succeeded.

It is the same with your meditation. If you had gone just
a bit higher or deeper, you would have had your experience. But your attention was diverted or something
made you pull back instead of going on. You failed to
maintain your aspiration, and your consciousness fell.
It is as if you were climbing up to the highest branch of
a tree, but all of a sudden somebody called you from

below and you forgot about the delicious fruit at the top of the tree and climbed down. If you can maintain your height and not respond to any call or pull from below, then you will reach your highest, and you will get your experience.

While you are praying and meditating, imagine that you are riding a bicycle. When you ride a bicycle, the wheels have to be turning all the time. You cannot balance motionless at one point. While you are meditating you have to aspire all the time; otherwise, you will fall. In the spiritual life, movement has to be constant. Either you move forward or you move backward. If you try to remain motionless, the ignorance of the world will pull you back to your starting point.

In your life of aspiration what you need is not success but progress. Progress itself is the active form of success. When you start meditating early in the morning, if you think, 'Today I have to get the highest experience, or I will feel miserable," then God may give you the experience, which you will call success. But He will not utilise You as His instrument, because you are already trying to get something from Him. You are demanding that He give you an inner experience, whereas you should be asking only for the opportunity and privilege of being His instrument to serve Him in His own way.

If you cry only to please God in His own way, if you cry only for progress, then you are bound to get all the experiences which God has in store for you, at God's own time. Right now you are trying to climb up to a great height in order to get an experience. It is extremely difficult for you to go to that height at this stage of your spiritual development. But it is very easy for God to bring the fruit down and give it to you. He is an excellent climber; He can climb up and climb down. So if you can please God, even if you remain at the foot of the tree, God will climb up on your behalf and bring the experience down, if it is His Will that you have it.

Q Oftentimes I have the feeling or sensation that I see light, but my mind doubts it very forcefully. I was wondering if the light I see is real or imaginary.

A If it is real light, if it is pure, divine light, then rest assured that your mind cannot doubt what you are seeing. The mind does not have the capacity to doubt divine light while you are seeing it. The effulgence of light is such that it will not allow any mental suspicion or doubt to enter. When the real divine light appears, at that time the mind is obliterated; it does not function at all. The entire being becomes all soul.

The mind does have the capacity to doubt divine light afterwards. When you are seeing the light, the mind is divine. After, when your consciousness descends and you are no longer physically aware of the light, the mind can gather strength and try to throw suspicion into your experience. Then you may doubt the light that you saw. If right now God stands before you, you are not going to doubt Him. But the moment God disappears from your outer vision, you can doubt God.

Because of your oneness with your body, you don't doubt your eyes or your nose. You know that they are part and parcel of your body and that your body is part and parcel of your life. Similarly, divine light is part and parcel of your real existence. How can you deny or doubt your own existence? But after the experience is over and you no longer feel the light as your own, at that time doubt may enter into you.

Q I once had an experience in which I felt the purity of God and the power and Eternity of God, but then the feeling left me.

A This was a gift of pure Grace. The Supreme, out of His infinite bounty, unconditionally offered His Grace to you. That is why this experience was possible. These things are not hallucinations. Spiritual Masters have a free access to these experiences, but seekers also can have them if they pray and meditate sincerely.

You got this experience because of God's Grace, but impurity did not allow you to keep it. Any spiritual wealth that you may have, no matter what kind it is, will be destroyed by impurity. Many people have good experiences on certain days, but the next day they indulge in lower vital life. Then all their higher experiences are destroyed. But if we refrain from enjoying vital life and emotional life, then our higher experiences grow. They grow and become very solid, like a banyan tree. So you have to be extremely careful not to indulge in the vital life if you want to retain the power of your highest experiences.

Q In meditation I have had the experience that I was totally free. But then I had to go back to my regular life, and I felt very tired and very drained.

A When you get a higher experience, it is something that will nourish you, feed you and strengthen you. If you are exhausted, if your energy is drained, it means that you have pulled beyond your capacity. Otherwise, right after meditation, you will have the strength of a lion.

Q When I am meditating well and I start to go deep within, after a few minutes I feel sleepy and my whole body goes almost numb.

A You are having the experience of silence. During your meditation your mind has totally surrendered to your heart, and the heart and the mind have both surrendered to the soul. At that time you get a feeling of static silence. Mentally you feel that you are not in this world, and that you have to come back and be very dynamic. But no! At that time the soul is operating most powerfully, and you do not have to create any movement.

This world of silence is not like ordinary sleep, where one becomes totally unconscious. On the contrary, it is a very good state. In the silence itself there is spontaneous creativity, spontaneous movement and spontaneous life—the life of spiritual awakening and spiritual revelation. Try to remain there and grow into that state with utmost sincerity, humility and devotion. You can stay there for a few days or even a month without any fear. Then you will see that the static silence will grow into dynamic silence.

If you feel sleepy when you are merely preparing to meditate, it means that inertia and lethargy are present. But if this feeling comes during a good meditation, it is not sleep at all. You are entering into the world of silence and mistaking it for sleep.

Q When I first started meditating, I had the feeling of purity and divinity flowing through each cell of my body. But now when I meditate I don't feel this, yet I think I have improved my meditation-capacity. Why is this?

A When you start to run your fastest, at the beginning you have so much alertness. Then, after thirty metres, your limbs get increased coordination. You feel totally relaxed and you may not even feel that you are running. You are not putting out any extra effort, but your speed is not slowing down. In the beginning your mind has to convince your body to move. But once you have entered into your natural stride, your mind no longer has to convince your body to run fast. You can run your fastest automatically.

Q On different occasions I have seen red, blue and white light during meditation. Could you please explain the significance of these?

A Red is the dynamic aspect of God; it represents the divine power which you are seeing inside yourself. When divinity's power enters into you, you are energised.

White is the colour of purity. It represents the consciousness of the Divine Mother. When you see white all around you, you feel that your whole physical existence is inundated with purity, from the soles of your feet to the crown of your head.

When you see a pale blue colour, it means that Infinity is entering into your aspiring consciousness. You cannot understand Infinity with your mind. The mind will imagine a great distance, expand it a little farther and then stop. But Infinity goes on expanding forever. When you see blue, try to feel that your consciousness is expanding into Infinity and that Infinity is entering into your aspiring consciousness.

Each prayer is divinely important. Each meditation is supremely significant. Each experience is soulfully fruitful.

Q I used to feel and see a golden light around my heart, but now I no longer do. How can I regain this wonderful presence?

A When this golden light, which is the light of divine manifestation, touches earth, it may not be able to remain for long. If it feels that it cannot remain in the heart because the heart is not pure enough, it will recede. But when the heart is pure, this light functions first in the heart region; then it moves into the vital and the physical.

Understanding Your Inner Experiences

To regain the visible presence of light is not necessary. If you want to follow a spiritual path, it is not the light that you want—it is God's constant concern for you, God's real love and blessing. When you have God's concern it can take the form of light, peace, power or any divine quality.

When a beginner sees light, he feels that he is making extraordinary progress. To some extent it is true. If God shows you light, naturally you will be inspired to dive deep into the sea of spirituality. But if God feels that what you need is peace and not light, then He will act through you in a different way.

You want to regain the wonderful presence of this light, but you will not get utmost satisfaction from seeing this light, because you will not be fulfilling God in His own way. Your highest aim is to please God in His own way. When God gives you an experience, you should be most grateful to Him. And when He does not give you one, you have to be equally grateful, because He knows what is best for you. It is your business to meditate soulfully, and it is God's business to give you light or peace or power. God will give you what He has and what He is if you give Him what you have and what you are. What you have is ignorance, and what you are is aspiration. So my request to you is to please God in His own way and not care for the things which you once had and which you now feel you are missing.

Q Would you please speak about the aura seen in meditation?

A Each individual human being has an aura. You may see your aura during your meditation, but you may also see it during concentration or even during sleep. There is no direct connection between meditation and the aura except that while you are meditating you may enter into a more peaceful consciousness, where it becomes easier for you to see an aura.

Q I have recently felt quite distinctly a force that people throw around themselves for protection, or when they don't want to speak to someone. It is like a solid object, like a wall. Is it built consciously or unconsciously?

A Usually it is built consciously. Some seekers feel that when they are around unaspiring people they need protection to maintain their high consciousness. They are afraid that the consciousness of the unaspiring people will enter into them like arrows and destroy their aspiration, so they consciously build a wall around themselves. Sometimes ordinary people who are not aspiring have a tremendous insecurity, so they also build a wall around themselves. They are afraid that others will take away whatever little wealth they have.

Spiritual Masters may build this wall to protect themselves from the attacks of the world around them. Some people who come into the presence of a spiritual Master do not want to accept anything. The moment the Master wants to give them peace or light, they attack him inwardly. Or people come to a Master without knowing what they want. Then, for example, when peace, light or bliss is offered, they feel that it is something strange, something foreign, so they reject it vehemently. Or they come to the Master with tremendous expectation and demand, saying "Give me, give me, give me!" But when the Master gives them what they need, they are not satisfied, so they attack him inwardly. For these reasons the Master creates a kind of shield for self-protection.

Each individual has a special aura of which he is not conscious. That aura goes around the person from head to foot and consciously protects him. When we meditate we may see that there is an aura constantly revolving around us. Others' auras we may also see, as people used to see them behind the Buddha or the Christ, for example. Usually these do not revolve or move. But the aura that we all have is constantly moving around us. This aura is a strong protection on the physical, vital and mental levels, but it does not protect the whole being. This aura becomes powerful only through prayer and meditation. Each day when we pray and meditate, this aura is strengthened; then it moves very, very fast. When the movement becomes extremely fast, the aura acquires tremendous strength, and at that time it is able to protect the entire being.

Q When I meditate I often feel a split in my consciousness. Part of my consciousness is in a deep meditation while another part of my consciousness is observing and carrying on a running commentary on what is being experienced. What does that mean?

A There should be no split in your consciousness. When you are properly meditating, your consciousness will become a single entity. If you feel that you are making a running commentary, then you have to know that either your mind or your vital or your physical is not totally one with your meditation. Your heart and soul are meditating most devotedly, but the mind may not be there. In our path we give more importance to the heart than to the mind. But that does not mean that we can neglect or ignore the mind. The mind has to become one with the heart so that the soul can carry both of them together. When you are meditating, sometimes your mind does not want to sit beside the heart or become one with it. That is why you are aware of this split in your consciousness. It comes from the mind. In your case very rarely does it come from the vital.

One of the Upanishads mentions that there are three kinds of meditation: gross meditation, subtle meditation and transcendental meditation. Your particular experience takes place in the first stage. In spite of having a very high meditation, you feel that your whole existence is not there. Although in your psychic consciousness you are having a very high meditation, it will not be totally fruitful, because all the members of your inner family are not participating.

In the second stage of meditation you will see that you have become totally aware of and unified in your consciousness. Now you are just using the term 'consciousness', but in that stage you will actually be able to see and feel what consciousness is. At every moment you will be able to see the divine streak of light, the all-pervading light inside you which has united you with the Highest. In this stage of meditation you become the connecting link between earth and Heaven.

The third and highest stage of meditation is transcendental meditation. In this stage you will be able to feel or see yourself as both the meditator and the meditation itself. In this stage the seer and the seen come together. This happens only in the highest Transcendental Consciousness when you go beyond nature's dance, which means temptation, frustration, anxiety, fear, jealousy, failure and so forth. But all this does not mean that in gross meditation you cannot enter into your deepest meditation. You can. But only your heart and your soul will enjoy the deepest meditation; the physical, the vital and the mind will not be able to enjoy the deepest meditation at that time. That is why it is called gross.

Q I once felt during meditation that my soul came out of the body.

A The soul can come out of the body during meditation. In some cases the soul comes to the fore so powerfully that the physical consciousness either leaves or becomes submerged or totally illumined and transformed by the soul's light.

Q While meditating I sometimes feel that my body is moving rhythmically, but when I open my eyes I see that I am not moving at all.

A The movement you feel is in the inner world, in your subtle body. That reality has not yet manifested itself in the physical, nor does it need to. If you feel that you are flying while you are meditating, you do not have to manifest this movement in the physical.

But if you feel abundant peace within you, then you should immediately try to manifest it in your eyes, in your physical consciousness. Here on earth very few people have peace. When you bring peace into the outer world and manifest it, you are solving the problems of the entire world. The world needs peace, the world needs love, the world needs all divine qualities. Your goal is to see and feel peace, light and bliss, and bring them to the fore in your outer life. By manifesting these divine qualities, you can serve mankind and fulfil God.

Q When meditating, inside I feel very strong and outside I feel very soft. But as I go deeper, I start expanding. What does that signify?

A That is excellent. You feel strong inside because you are bringing down divine peace, light and bliss into your system. The more you consciously and devotedly bring down these divine forces, the stronger you become inwardly. And these blessings from above are helping you to expand your consciousness.

Outwardly you are feeling soft, but this is not actually softness. It is inner peace and inner confidence that are growing in your outer being. When you have boundless inner strength, you do not have to display it outwardly. You do not have to clench your fists. You are relaxed because your inner strength has given you confidence. You are like a divine hero. At any moment you know you can defeat your enemy or surmount any obstruction, so you are outwardly relaxed.

 There is nothing is more powerful than peace.

Q Sometimes after meditation I touch things and find that they are not solid; they are fluid. They lose their solid state. What does this mean?

A Actually they do not lose their solid state. After a deep meditation, when you touch a wall or some other solid object, if you feel that it is soft and that you can penetrate it, you have to know that your consciousness has become identified with the consciousness of your surroundings. When you have come out of a deep meditation and touch something, you can feel your own consciousness in that thing. The solid object has accepted you and embraced you; it has opened its heart's door to become one with you.

When I touch someone from my highest consciousness, that person may not be in his highest consciousness. His mind may be roaming here and there. But if I consciously identify myself with that person, immediately I can enter into and become one with that person's consciousness.

Q When I meditate, I enter into the inner world and sometimes I see things which materialise in the outer world after a few months. Should I try to transcend this?

A What you are doing is entering into the soul's world. You do not have to try to transcend this; there is no necessity. However, you should be aware of whether or not you are crying to know these things. If you are meditating with a view to finding out what is going to happen in the future, then you do have to transcend this. If you say during your meditation, "O God, tell me what is going to happen to my husband or my son," it is a mistake. But if you are only trying to go deep within to have a profound meditation, then I can say that God wants to show you these things for a divine purpose. You should not try to transcend these experiences because, in that case, it is God's Will that you are fulfilling, and not your own desire.

Q When I meditate, I see within and without that everything is alive and has millions of patterns. I see something like a living presence in everything. Could you comment on this?

A Inside everything is God. And where God is present, life is bound to be present. Where there is life, there is God, and where there is God, there is life. Inside one thing you are seeing many varieties. The One is being expressed in many forms and many patterns. When you look at a lotus you see one flower, but it is expressed or manifested by many petals, and by leaves, the stem and other parts. In a lotus you see the manifestation of oneness through various forms. You touch one particular part of the lotus, the leaf, for example, and you say, "This is the lotus." Then you touch the stem, and again you say, "This is the lotus." God is there in all parts of the flower; that is why you feel that each part is the whole. God is present wherever life exists. God is endless in expression. He is endless in manifestation.

Q At times during meditation, I feel that my physical heart stops for a few seconds. This frightens me.

A When you feel that the physical heart stops, this is a very good experience. But you must not be afraid of it; you won't die. It means that the physical in you has totally surrendered to the spiritual in you. Many spiritual Masters, in order to enter into the higher regions during meditation, have consciously stopped their heartbeat. But only Yogis and spiritual Masters can do this at will. Out of His infinite Compassion, God has given you a glimpse of this experience. You should be very happy. When you become a Yogi, it will be up to you whether or not you want to stop your heartbeat during meditation. What it means is that the physical has totally ceased and the spiritual is reigning supreme. At that time you do not need the physical.

Q When I am meditating, I feel my head expanding, and I feel that something is pounding the top of my head.

A Two seemingly contradictory things are happening. On the one hand, you feel that your head is expanding. This is the purified consciousness that is expanding in your mind. On the other hand, your impure consciousness is trying to pull down light from above by force. When it does this, you feel a heavy pressure.

When the pure forces in us want to bring down something from above, there is no pressure. When our little divinity looks up and invites the highest divinity to enter, it sees its oneness with the Highest. It is like a child who sees his father. The child is not afraid because he knows this is his own father. He calls his father, and his father comes to him. But if he invites someone else's father, he may be afraid of that person. He may fear that that man will show him an angry face and say, "Why did you call me?" Because that person is unfamiliar, the child experiences a kind of uneasiness and fear.

Similarly, when the impure mind invites the highest divinity to descend, the divinity is ready to come, but the impure mind is afraid. It thinks it will be crushed. It does not get any familiar feeling. But the divine in us does get a familiar feeling when it sees the highest divinity coming down. It is the undivine in us that is always afraid of the divine, even though at times it wants to see the divine. It feels uneasy, and this gives us a severe pressure in the head.

Above the toil of life my soul is a bird of fire winging the Infinite.

Samadhi: The Height of Divine Consciousness

Samadhi: The Height of Divine Consciousness

❦ What Is Samadhi?

Samadhi is a spiritual state of consciousness. There are various kinds of samadhi. Among the minor samadhis, *savikalpa* samadhi happens to be the highest. Beyond *savikalpa* comes *nirvikalpa* samadhi, but there is a great gulf between these two: they are two radically different samadhis. Again, there is something even beyond *nirvikalpa* samadhi called *sahaja* samadhi.

In *savikalpa* samadhi, for a short period of time you lose all human consciousness. In this state the conception of time and space is altogether different. For an hour or two hours you are completely in another world. You see there that almost everything is done. Here in this world there are many desires still unfulfilled in yourself and in others. Millions of desires are not fulfilled, and millions of things remain to be done. But when you are in *savikalpa* samadhi, you see that practically everything is done; you have nothing to do. You are only an instrument. If you are used, well and good; otherwise, things are all done. But from *savikalpa* samadhi everybody has to return to ordinary consciousness.

Even in *savikalpa* samadhi there are grades. Just as there are brilliant students and poor students in the same class in school, so also in *savikalpa* samadhi some aspirants reach the highest grade, while less aspiring seekers reach a lower rung of the ladder, where everything is not so clear and vivid as on the highest level.

In *savikalpa* samadhi there are thoughts and ideas coming from various places, but they do not affect you. While you are meditating, you remain undisturbed, and your inner being functions in a dynamic and confident manner. But when you are a little higher, when you have become one with the soul in *nirvikalpa* samadhi, there will be no ideas or thoughts at all. I am trying to explain it in words, but the consciousness of *nirvikalpa* samadhi can never be adequately explained or expressed. I am trying my best to tell you about this from a very high consciousness, but still my mind is expressing it. But in *nirvikalpa* samadhi there is no mind; there is only infinite peace and bliss. There nature's dance stops, and the knower and the known become one. There you enjoy a supremely divine, all-pervading, self-amorous ecstasy. You become the object of enjoyment, you become the enjoyer and you become the enjoyment itself.

When you enter into *nirvikalpa* samadhi, the first thing you feel is that your heart is larger than the universe itself. Ordinarily you see the world around you, and the universe seems infinitely larger than you are. But this is because the world and the universe are perceived by the limited mind. When you are in *nirvikalpa* samadhi, you see the universe as a tiny dot inside your vast heart.

In *nirvikalpa* samadhi there is infinite bliss. Bliss is a vague word to most people. They hear that there is something called bliss, and some people say that they have experienced it, but most individuals have no first-hand knowledge of it. When you enter into *nirvikalpa* samadhi, however, you not only feel bliss, but actually grow into that bliss.

The third thing you feel in *nirvikalpa* samadhi is power. All the power of all the occultists put together is nothing compared with the power you have in *nirvikalpa* samadhi. But the power that you can take from samadhi to utilise on earth is infinitesimal compared with the entirety.

Nirvikalpa samadhi is the highest samadhi that most realised spiritual Masters attain. It lasts for a few hours or a few days, and then one has to come down. When one comes down, what happens? Very often one forgets his own name and age; one cannot speak or think properly. But through continued practice, gradually one becomes able to come down from *nirvikalpa* samadhi and immediately function in a normal way.

Generally, when one enters into *nirvikalpa* samadhi, one does not want to come back into the world again. If one stays there for eighteen or twenty-one days, there is every possibility that the soul will leave the body for good. There were spiritual Masters in the hoary past who attained *nirvikalpa* samadhi and did not come down. They attained their highest samadhi, but found it impossible to enter into the world atmosphere again and work like human beings. One cannot operate in the world while in that state of consciousness; it is simply impossible. But there is a divine dispensation. If the Supreme wants a particular soul to work here on earth, even after twenty-one or twenty-two days, the Supreme can take that individual into another channel of dynamic, divine consciousness and have him return to the earth-plane to act.

Sahaja samadhi is by far the highest type of samadhi. In this samadhi one is in the highest consciousness but, at the same time, one is able to work in the gross physical world. One maintains the experience of *nirvikalpa* samadhi while simultaneously entering into earthly activities. One has become the soul and, at the same time, is utilising the body as a perfect instrument. In *sahaja* samadhi one does the usual things that an ordinary human being does. But in the inmost recesses of the heart one is surcharged with divine illumination. When one has this *sahaja* samadhi, one becomes the Lord and Master of Reality. One can go at his sweet will to the Highest and then come down to the earth-consciousness to manifest.

Even after achieving the highest type of realisation, on very rare occasions is anyone blessed with *sahaja* samadhi. Very few spiritual Masters have achieved this state. For *sahaja* samadhi, the Supreme's infinite Grace is required. *Sahaja* samadhi comes only when one has established inseparable oneness with the Supreme, or when one wants to show, on rare occasions, that he is the Supreme. He who has achieved *sahaja* samadhi and remains in this samadhi, consciously and perfectly manifests God at every second, and is thus the greatest pride of the Transcendental Supreme.

Q&A

Q In the highest state of samadhi, when you look at other human beings, what kind of consciousness do you feel in them?

A When one is in the highest transcendental samadhi, the physical personality of others disappears. We do not see others as human beings. We see only a flow of consciousness, like a river that is entering into the ocean. He who is in the highest trance becomes the ocean, and he who is in a lower state of consciousness is the river. The river flows into the sea and becomes one with the sea. The one who is enjoying the highest samadhi does not notice any individuality or personality in others. A human being who is not in this state of samadhi is a flowing river of consciousness, while the one who is in samadhi has become the sea itself, the sea of peace and light.

Q Do you teach your disciples any specific technique for attaining samadhi?

A No. Samadhi is a very high state of consciousness. If the beginner comes to kindergarten and asks the teacher how he can study for his Master's degree, the teacher will simply laugh. He will say, "How can I tell you?" Before we are ready to try to attain samadhi, we have to go through many, many, many inner spiritual experiences. Then there comes a time when the Master sees that the student is ready to enter into *savikalpa* samadhi. *Nirvikalpa* samadhi is out of the question for seekers right now. One has to be a most advanced seeker before he can even think of attaining *savikalpa* samadhi. *Nirvikalpa* samadhi one gets only in the highest stage of aspiration. Unfortunately, I do not have anyone among my disciples now whom I can help to enter into that state. I am very proud of my disciples. Some are very sincere and devoted, and are making very fast progress; but the time has yet to come for them to think of entering into samadhi. For all seekers I wish to say that the spiritual ladder has quite a few rungs. We have to climb up one step at a time. Samadhi, for my disciples and for the vast majority of spiritual seekers on earth, is a far cry right now.

Index

Exercises, see techniques;
> before meditation, 154

Expansion, feeling of, 254

Expectation, 47-48

Experience(s) 55, 235-255

Eyes, position in meditation, 21-22, 130, 233

F

Falling asleep, 21-22, 123-126, 154

Fasting, 28

Fatigue, 152-153

Fear, 126, 128, 188-189;
> of giving up old life, 227;
> of Sri Chinmoy's picture, 226-227;
> technique to remove, 23, 193

Fixed time for meditation, 148-150, 152-155

Flame, meditation on, 19-20, 36-37, 188

Flower(s), concentration on, 72;
> meditation on, 73;
> use in meditation, 19, 27

Folding hands, 231

Forgiveness, 131

Friendship with divine qualities, 15-16, 138

Frustration, 160, 192-193

G

Garden, visualisation technique, 12

God, 13-14, 28;
> belief in, 7;
> oneness with, 6;
> presence of the One in many, 253

Gods and goddesses, pictures of, 224

God's name, repeating, 24, 111, 124, 193, 219

God's presence in others, 142, 159-160, 199, 204

God's Will, 48, 83-84, 86-89, 205, 238-239

Golden being, visualisation technique, 74;

contemplation technique, 75
Grace, 121, 243-244
Gratitude, 133, 139, 169, 174, 219;
     and prayer, 88;
     and receptivity, 109-110;
     technique to increase, 73
Group meditation, see collective meditation
Guru, 209-216, see also Master

H

Habits, how to break, 190
Hands folded, 231
Hatha Yoga, 21, 154
Headache, 127-30
Healing, 190-191
Heart, 45-46, 51-59,;
     -centre, 22, 53, 66;
     concentration on, 71, 130;
     emptying, 7;
     meditating in, 12-13, 127-129, 233-234
Heartbeat, concentration on, 72
     stopping, 254
Height and depth in meditation, 55-57
Helping others, 194-195
Housewife, advice for, 159-169
How long to meditate, 132, 145, 156-159, 162-163
Humanity, 200-201, 204
Humility, technique to increase, 73

I

Identification, 51-52
Illumination, 82, 206-207, 211
Imagination, 170
Impurity, 127, 244
Incense, use in meditation, 19, 27
Individual meditation, 20

R

S

V-Z

About Sri Chinmoy

Sri Chinmoy is a fully realised spiritual Master dedicated to inspiring and serving those seeking a deeper meaning in life. Through his teaching of meditation, lectures and writings, and through his own life of dedicated service to humanity, he tries to show others how to find inner peace and fulfilment.

Born in Bengal in 1931, Sri Chinmoy entered an ashram (spiritual community) at the age of 12. His life of intense spiritual practice included meditating for up to 14 hours a day, together with writing poetry, essays and devotional songs, doing selfless service and practising athletics. While still in his early teens, he had many profound inner experiences and attained spiritual realisation. He remained in the ashram for 20 years, deepening and expanding his realisation, and in 1964 came to New York City to share his inner wealth with sincere seekers.

Today, Sri Chinmoy serves as a spiritual guide to disciples in some 80 centres around the world. He teaches the "Path of the Heart," which he feels is the simplest way to make rapid spiritual progress. By meditating on the spiritual heart, he teaches, the seeker can discover his own inner treasures of peace, joy, light and love. The role of a spiritual Master, according to Sri Chinmoy, is to help the seeker live so that these inner riches can illumine his life. He instructs his disciples in the inner life and elevates their consciousness not only beyond their expectation, but even beyond their imagination.

In return he asks his students to meditate regularly and to try to nurture the inner qualities he brings to the fore in them.

Sri Chinmoy teaches that love is the most direct way for a seeker to approach the Supreme. When a child feels love for his father, it does not matter how great the father is in the world's eye; through his love the child feels only his oneness with his father and his father's possessions. This same approach, applied to the Supreme, permits the seeker to feel that the Supreme and His own Eternity, Infinity and Immortality are the seeker's own. This philosophy of love, Sri Chinmoy feels, expresses the deepest bond between man and God, who are aspects of the same unified consciousness. In the life-game, man fulfils himself in the Supreme by realising that God is man's own highest self. The Supreme reveals Himself through man, who serves as His instrument for world transformation and perfection.

Sri Chinmoy's path does not end with realisation. Once we realise the highest, it is still necessary to manifest this reality in the world around us. In Sri Chinmoy's words, "To climb up the mango tree is great, but it is not enough. We have to climb down again to distribute the mangoes and make the world aware of their significance. Until we do this, our role is not complete and God will not be satisfied or fulfilled."

In the traditional Indian fashion, Sri Chinmoy does not charge a fee for his spiritual guidance, nor does he charge for his frequent lectures, concerts or public meditations. His only fee, he says, is the seeker's sincere inner cry. He takes a personal interest in each of his students, and when he accepts a disciple, he takes full responsibility for that seeker's inner progress. In New York, Sri Chinmoy meditates in person with his disciples several times a week and offers a regular

Wednesday evening meditation session for the general public. Students living outside New York see Sri Chinmoy during worldwide gatherings that take place three times a year, during visits to New York, or during the Master's frequent trips to their cities. They find that the inner bond between Master and disciple transcends physical separation.

As part of his selfless offering to humanity, Sri Chinmoy conducts peace meditations twice each week for ambassadors and staff at United Nations headquarters in New York. He also conducts peace meditations for government officials at the United States Congress in Washington, D.C., and recently he was invited to inaugurate a regular series of meditations at the British Parliament.

In addition, Sri Chinmoy leads an active life, demonstrating most vividly that spirituality is not an escape from the world, but a means of transforming it. He has written more than 700 books, which include plays, poems, stories, essays, commentaries and answers to questions on spirituality. He has painted thousands of widely exhibited mystical paintings and composed more than 6,000 devotional songs.

Sri Chinmoy accepts students at all levels of development, from beginners to advanced seekers, and lovingly guides them inwardly and outwardly according to their individual needs.

For further information, please write to:

AUM PUBLICATIONS
86-24 Parsons Blvd.
Jamaica, N.Y. 11432